The Merchant of Venice

William Shakespeare

First Folio

Demetra Publishing

Bulgaria

First published in 1605
Cover Image: Piazza San Marco
Artist: Canaletto
License: CC0 1.0 Universal (CC0 1.0)
ISBN: 9781096110422

CONTENTS

DRAMATIS PERSONAE

The Duke of Venice
The Prince of Morocco,
The Prince of Arragon, suitors to Portia
Antonio, a merchant of Venice
Bassanio, his friend, suitor to Portia
Solanio
Gratiano
Salerio, friends to Antonio and Bassanio
Lorenzo, in love with Jessica
Shylock, a rich Jew
Tubal, a Jew, his friend
Launcelot Gobbo, a clown, servant to Shylock
Old Gobbo, father to Launcelot
Leonardo, servant to Bassanio
Balthazar
Stephano, servants to Portia
Portia, a rich heiress, of Belmont
Nerissa, her waiting-gentlewoman
Jessica, daughter to Shylock
Magnificoes of Venice, Officers of the Court of Justice,
Jailer, Servants to Portia, and other Attendants

SCENE

Partly at Venice and partly at Belmont, the seat of Portia

ACT I

SCENE I

Enter Antonio, Salerio, and Solanio.

Antonio.
In sooth, I know not why I am so sad;
It wearies me, you say it wearies you;
But how I caught it, found it, or came by it,
What stuff 'tis made of, whereof it is born,
I am to learn;
And such a want-wit sadness makes of me,
That I have much ado to know myself.

Salerio.
Your mind is tossing on the ocean,
There where your argosies with portly sail
Like signiors and rich burghers on the flood,
Or as it were the pageants of the sea,
Do overpeer the petty traffickers
That cur'sy to them, do them reverence,
As they fly by them with their woven wings.

Solanio.
Believe me, sir, had I such venture forth,

The better part of my affections would
Be with my hopes abroad. I should be still
Plucking the grass to know where sits the wind,
Piring in maps for ports and piers and roads;
And every object that might make me fear
Misfortune to my ventures, out of doubt
Would make me sad.

Salerio.
My wind cooling my broth
Would blow me to an ague when I thought
What harm a wind too great might do at sea.
I should not see the sandy hour-glass run
But I should think of shallows and of flats,
And see my wealthy Andrew [dock'd] in sand,
Vailing her high top lower than her ribs
To kiss her burial. Should I go to church
And see the holy edifice of stone,
And not bethink me straight of dangerous rocks,
Which touching but my gentle vessel's side
Would scatter all her spices on the stream,
Enrobe the roaring waters with my silks,
And in a word, but even now worth this,
And now worth nothing? Shall I have the thought
To think on this, and shall I lack the thought
That such a thing bechanc'd would make me sad?
But tell not me; I know Antonio
Is sad to think upon his merchandise.

Antonio.
Believe me, no. I thank my fortune for it,
My ventures are not in one bottom trusted,
Nor to one place; nor is my whole estate
Upon the fortune of this present year:
45 Therefore my merchandise makes me not sad.

Solanio.
Why then you are in love.

Antonio.
Fie, fie!

Solanio.

Not in love neither? Then let us say you are sad
Because you are not merry; and 'twere as easy
For you to laugh and leap, and say you are merry
Because you not sad. Now by two-headed Janus,
Nature hath fram'd strange fellows in her time:
Some that will evermore peep through their eyes,
And laugh like parrots at a bagpiper;
And other of such vinegar aspect
That they'll not show their teeth in way of smile
Though Nestor swear the jest be laughable.

Enter Bassanio, Lorenzo, and Gratiano.
Here comes Bassanio, your most noble kinsman,
Gratiano, and Lorenzo. Fare ye well,
We leave you now with better company.

sarcasm?

Salerio.

I would have stay'd till I had made you merry,
If worthier friends had not prevented me.

Antonio.

Your worth is very dear in my regard.
I take it your own business calls on you,
And you embrace th' occasion to depart.

Salerio.

Good morrow, my good lords.

Bassanio.

Good signiors both, when shall we laugh? say, when?
You grow exceeding strange. Must it be so?

Salerio.

We'll make our leisures to attend on yours.

Exeunt Salerio and Solanio.

Lorenzo.

My Lord Bassanio, since you have found Antonio,
We two will leave you, but at dinner-time
I pray you have in mind where we must meet.

Bassanio.

I will not fail you.

Gratiano.

You look not well, Signior Antonio,
You have too much respect upon the world.
They lose it that do buy it with much care.
Believe me you are marvellously chang'd.

Antonio.

I hold the world but as the world, Gratiano,
A stage, where every man must play a part,
And mine a sad one.

Gratiano.

Let me play the fool,
With mirth and laughter let old wrinkles come,
And let my liver rather heat with wine
Than my heart cool with mortifying groans.
Why should a man, whose blood is warm within,
Sit like his grandsire cut in alablaster?
Sleep when he wakes? and creep into the jaundies
By being peevish? I tell thee what, Antonio—
I love thee, and 'tis my love that speaks—
There are a sort of men whose visages
Do cream and mantle like a standing pond,
And do a willful stillness entertain,
With purpose to be dress'd in an opinion
Of wisdom, gravity, profound conceit,
As who should say, "I am Sir Oracle,
And when I ope my lips let no dog bark!"
O my Antonio, I do know of these
That therefore only are reputed wise
For saying nothing; when I am very sure
If they should speak, would almost damn those ears
Which hearing them would call their brothers fools.
I'll tell thee more of this another time;
But fish not with this melancholy bait
For this fool gudgeon, this opinion.
Come, good Lorenzo. Fare ye well a while,
I'll end my exhortation after dinner.

Lorenzo.

Well, we will leave you then till dinner-time.
I must be one of these same dumb wise men,

[handwritten margin note: man who don't speak]

For Gratiano never lets me speak.

Gratiano.
Well, keep me company but two years moe,
Thou shalt not know the sound of thine own tongue.

Antonio.
Fare you well! I'll grow a talker for this gear.

Gratiano.
Thanks, i' faith, for silence is only commendable
In a neat's tongue dried and a maid not vendible.

Exeunt [Gratiano and Lorenzo].

Antonio. It is that—any thing now!

Bassanio. Gratiano speaks an infinite deal of nothing, more than any man in all Venice. His reasons are as two grains of wheat hid in two bushels of chaff; you shall seek all day ere you find them, and when you have them, they are not worth the search.

Antonio.
Well, tell me now what lady is the same
To whom you swore a secret pilgrimage,
That you to-day promis'd to tell me of?

Bassanio.
'Tis not unknown to you, Antonio,
How much I have disabled mine estate,
By something showing a more swelling port
Than my faint means would grant continuance.
Nor do I now make moan to be abridg'd
From such a noble rate, but my chief care
Is to come fairly off from the great debts
Wherein my time something too prodigal
Hath left me gag'd. To you, Antonio,
I owe the most in money and in love,
And from your love I have a warranty
To unburthen all my plots and purposes
How to get clear of all the debts I owe.

Antonio.
I pray you, good Bassanio, let me know it,

[handwritten margin notes: "all about money", "economic terms", "money comes first"]

And if it stand, as you yourself still do,
Within the eye of honor, be assur'd
My purse, my person, my extremest means,
Lie all unlock'd to your occasions.

Bassanio.

In my school-days, when I had lost one shaft,
I shot his fellow of the self-same flight
The self-same way with more advised watch
To find the other forth, and by adventuring both
I oft found both. I urge this childhood proof,
Because what follows is pure innocence.
I owe you much, and like a willful youth,
That which I owe is lost, but if you please
To shoot another arrow that self way
Which you did shoot the first, I do not doubt,
As I will watch the aim, or to find both
Or bring your latter hazard back again,
And thankfully rest debtor for the first.

Antonio.

You know me well, and herein spend but time
To wind about my love with circumstance,
And out of doubt you do me now more wrong
In making question of my uttermost
Than if you had made waste of all I have.
Then do but say to me what I should do
That in your knowledge may by me be done,
And I am prest unto it; therefore speak.

Bassanio.

In Belmont is a lady richly left,
And she is fair and, fairer than that word,
Of wondrous virtues. Sometimes from her eyes
I did receive fair speechless messages.
Her name is Portia, nothing undervalu'd
To Cato's daughter, Brutus' Portia.
Nor is the wide world ignorant of her worth,
For the four winds blow in from every coast
Renowned suitors, and her sunny locks
Hang on her temples like a golden fleece,
Which makes her seat of Belmont Colchis' strond,

And many Jasons come in quest of her.
O my Antonio, had I but the means
To hold a rival place with one of them,
I have a mind presages me such thrift
That I should questionless be fortunate!

Antonio.
Thou know'st that all my fortunes are at sea,
Neither have I money nor commodity
To raise a present sum; therefore go forth,
Try what my credit can in Venice do.
That shall be rack'd, even to the uttermost,
To furnish thee to Belmont, to fair Portia.
Go presently inquire, and so will I,
Where money is, and I no question make
To have it of my trust, or for my sake.

Exeunt.

Antonio is very loyal

SCENE II

Enter Portia with her waiting-woman, Nerissa.

Portia. By my troth, Nerissa, my little body is a-weary of this great world.

Nerissa. You would be, sweet madam, if your miseries were in the same abundance as your good fortunes are; and yet for aught I see, they are as sick that surfeit with too much as they that starve with nothing. It is no mean happiness therefore to be seated in the mean: superfluity comes sooner by white hairs, but competency lives longer.

Portia. Good sentences, and well pronounc'd.

Nerissa. They would be better if well follow'd.

doing good isn't easy

Portia. If to do were as easy as to know what were good to do, chapels had been churches, and poor men's cottages princes' palaces. It is a good divine that follows his own instructions; I can easier teach twenty what were good to be done, than to be one of the twenty to follow mine own teaching. The brain may devise laws for the blood, but a hot temper leaps o'er a cold decree—such a hare is madness the youth, to skip o'er the meshes of good counsel the cripple. But this reasoning is not in the fashion to choose me a husband. O me, the word choose! I may neither choose who I would, nor refuse who I dislike; so is the will of a living daughter curb'd by the will of a dead father. Is it not hard, Nerissa, that I cannot choose one, nor refuse none?

Nerissa. Your father was ever virtuous, and holy men at their death have good inspirations; therefore the lott'ry that he hath devis'd in these three chests of gold, silver, and lead, whereof who chooses his meaning chooses you, will no doubt never be chosen by any rightly but one who you shall rightly love. But what warmth is there in your affection towards any of these princely suitors that are already come?

Portia. I pray thee over-name them, and as thou namest them, I will describe them; and according to my description level at my affection.

Nerissa. First, there is the Neapolitan prince.

Portia. Ay, that's a colt indeed, for he doth nothing but talk of his horse, and he makes it a great appropriation to his own good parts that he can shoe him himself. I am much afeard my lady his mother play'd false with a smith.

Nerissa. Then is there the County Palentine.

Portia. He doth nothing but frown, as who should say, "And you will not have me, choose." He hears merry tales and smiles not. I fear he will prove the weeping philosopher when he grows old, being so full of unmannerly sadness in his youth. I had rather be married to a death's-head with a bone in his mouth than to either of these. God defend me from these two!

Nerissa. How say you by the French lord, Monsieur Le [Bon]?

Portia. God made him, and therefore let him pass for a man. In truth, I know it is a sin to be a mocker, but he! why, he hath a horse better than the Neapolitan's, a better bad habit of frowning than the Count Palentine; he is every man in no man. If a throstle sing, he falls straight a-cap'ring. He will fence with his own shadow. If I should marry him, I should marry twenty husbands. If he would despise me, I would forgive him, for if he love me to madness, I shall never requite him.

Nerissa. What say you then to Falconbridge, the young baron of England?

Portia. You know I say nothing to him, for he understands not me, nor I him. He hath neither Latin, French, nor Italian, and you will come into the court and swear that I have a poor pennyworth in the English. He is a proper man's picture, but alas, who can converse with a dumb show? How oddly he is suited! I think he bought his doublet in Italy, his round hose in France, his bonnet in Germany, and his behavior every where.

Nerissa. What think you of the Scottish lord, his neighbor?

Portia. That he hath a neighborly charity in him, for he borrow'd a box of the ear of the Englishman, and swore he would pay him again when he was able. I think the Frenchman became his surety and seal'd under for another.

Nerissa. How like you the young German, the Duke of Saxony's nephew?

Portia. Very vildly in the morning, when he is sober, and most vildly in the afternoon, when he is drunk. When he is best, he is a little worse than a man, and when he is worst, he is little better than a beast. And the worst fall that ever fell, I hope I shall make shift to go without him.

Nerissa. If he should offer to choose, and choose the right casket, you should refuse to perform your father's will, if you should refuse to accept him.

Portia. Therefore for fear of the worst, I pray thee set a deep glass of Rhenish wine on the contrary casket, for if the devil be within, and that temptation without, I know he will choose it. I will do any thing, Nerissa, ere I will be married to a spunge.

Nerissa. You need not fear, lady, the having any of these lords. They have acquainted me with their determinations, which is indeed to return to their home, and to trouble you with no more suit, unless you may be won by some other sort than your father's imposition depending on the caskets.

Portia. If I live to be as old as Sibylla, I will die as chaste as Diana, unless I be obtain'd by the manner of my father's will. I am glad this parcel of wooers are so reasonable, for there is not one among them but I dote on his very absence, and I pray God grant them a fair departure.

Nerissa. Do you not remember, lady, in your father's time, a Venetian, a scholar and a soldier, that came hither in company of the Marquis of Montferrat?

Portia. Yes, yes, it was Bassanio—as I think, so was he call'd.

Nerissa. True, madam; he, of all the men that ever my foolish eyes look'd upon, was the best deserving a fair lady.

Portia. I remember him well, and I remember him worthy of thy praise.

Enter a Servingman.

How now, what news?

Servingman. The four strangers seek for you, madam, to take their leave; and there is a forerunner come from a fift, the Prince of Morocco, who brings word the Prince his master will be here to-night.

Portia. If I could bid the fift welcome with so good heart as I can bid the other four farewell, I should be glad of his approach. If he have the condition of a saint, and the complexion of a devil, I had rather he should shrive me than wive me.
Come, Nerissa. Sirrah, go before.
Whiles we shut the gate upon one wooer, another knocks at the door.

Exeunt.

*comes
from Morocco
– complexion*

SCENE III

Enter Bassanio with Shylock the Jew.

Shylock. Three thousand ducats, well.

Bassanio. Ay, sir, for three months.

Shylock. For three months, well.

Bassanio. For the which, as I told you, Antonio shall be bound.

Shylock. Antonio shall become bound, well.

Bassanio. May you stead me? Will you pleasure me? Shall I know your answer?

Shylock. Three thousand ducats for three months, and Antonio bound.

Bassanio. Your answer to that.

Shylock. Antonio is a good man.

Jewish

Bassanio. Have you heard any imputation to the contrary?

Shylock. Ho, no, no, no, no! my meaning in saying he is a good man is to have you understand me that he is sufficient. Yet his means are in supposition: he hath an argosy bound to Tripolis, another to the Indies; I understand moreover upon the Rialto, he hath a third at Mexico, a fourth for England, and other ventures he hath, squand'red abroad. But ships are but boards, sailors but men; there be land-rats and water-rats, water-thieves and land- thieves, I mean pirates, and then there is the peril of waters, winds, and rocks. The man is notwithstanding sufficient. Three thousand ducats; I think I may take his bond.

Shylock doesn't like Antonio

Bassanio. Be assur'd you may.

Shylock. I will be assur'd I may; and that I may be assur'd, I will bethink me. May I speak with Antonio?

Bassanio. If it please you to dine with us.

Shylock. Yes, to smell pork, to eat of the habitation which your prophet the Nazarite conjur'd the devil into. I will buy with you, sell with you, talk with you, walk with you, and so following; but I will not eat with you, drink with you, nor pray with you. What news on the Rialto? Who is he comes here?

hates Christians

Enter Antonio.

Bassanio.
This is Signior Antonio.

Shylock. *[Aside.]*
How like a fawning publican he looks!
I hate him for he is a Christian; 39
But more, for that in low simplicity

wants to trick him

He lends out money gratis, and brings down 41
The rate of usance here with us in Venice.] 42
If I can catch him once upon the hip,
I will feed fat the ancient grudge I bear him.
He hates our sacred nation, and he rails
Even there where merchants most do congregate
On me, my bargains, and my well-won thrift,
Which he calls interest. Cursed be my tribe
If I forgive him!

Bassanio.
Shylock, do you hear?

Shylock.
I am debating of my present store,
And by the near guess of my memory,
I cannot instantly raise up the gross
Of full three thousand ducats. What of that?
Tubal, a wealthy Hebrew of my tribe,
Will furnish me. But soft, how many months
Do you desire?

[To Antonio.]
Rest you fair, good signior,
Your worship was the last man in our mouths.

Antonio.
Shylock, albeit I neither lend nor borrow
By taking nor by giving of excess,
Yet to supply the ripe wants of my friend,
I'll break a custom.

[To Bassanio.]
Is he yet possess'd
How much ye would?

Shylock.
Ay, ay, three thousand ducats.

Antonio.
And for three months.

Shylock.
I had forgot—three months—

[to Bassanio]

you told me so.
Well then, your bond; and let me see—but hear you,
Methoughts you said you neither lend nor borrow
Upon advantage.

Antonio.
I do never use it. — interest

Shylock. — money lender
When Jacob graz'd his uncle Laban's sheep—
This Jacob from our holy Abram was
(As his wise mother wrought in his behalf)
The third possessor; ay, he was the third—

Antonio.
And what of him? did he take interest?

Shylock.
No, not take interest, not as you would say
Directly int'rest. Mark what Jacob did:
When Laban and himself were compremis'd
That all the eanlings which were streak'd and pied
Should fall as Jacob's hire, the ewes being rank
In end of autumn turned to the rams,
And when the work of generation was
Between these woolly breeders in the act,
The skillful shepherd pill'd me certain wands,
And in the doing of the deed of kind,
He stuck them up before the fulsome ewes,
Who then conceiving did in eaning time
Fall parti-color'd lambs, and those were Jacob's.
This was a way to thrive, and he was blest;
And thrift is blessing, if men steal it not.

Antonio.
This was a venture, sir, that Jacob serv'd for,
A thing not in his power to bring to pass,
But sway'd and fashion'd by the hand of heaven.
Was this inserted to make interest good?
Or is your gold and silver ewes and rams?

Shylock.
I cannot tell, I make it breed as fast.

But note me, signior.

Antonio.
Mark you this, Bassanio,
The devil can cite Scripture for his purpose.
An evil soul producing holy witness
Is like a villain with a smiling cheek,
A goodly apple rotten at the heart.
O, what a goodly outside falsehood hath!

Shylock.
Three thousand ducats—'tis a good round sum.
Three months from twelve; then let me see, the rate—

Antonio.
Well, Shylock, shall we be beholding to you?

Shylock.
Signior Antonio, many a time and oft
In the Rialto you have rated me
About my moneys and my usances.
Still have I borne it with a patient shrug
(For suff'rance is the badge of all our tribe).
You call me misbeliever, cut-throat dog,
And spet upon my Jewish gaberdine,
And all for use of that which is mine own.
Well then, it now appears you need my help.
Go to then, you come to me, and you say,
"Shylock, we would have moneys," you say so—
You, that did void your rheum upon my beard,
And foot me as you spurn a stranger cur
Over your threshold; moneys is your suit.
What should I say to you? Should I not say,
"Hath a dog money? Is it possible
A cur can lend three thousand ducats?" Or
Shall I bend low and in a bondman's key,
With bated breath and whisp'ring humbleness,
Say this:
"Fair sir, you spet on me on Wednesday last,
You spurn'd me such a day, another time
You call'd me dog; and for these courtesies
I'll lend you thus much moneys"?

Antonio.
I am as like to call thee so again,
To spet on thee again, to spurn thee too.
If thou wilt lend this money, lend it not
As to thy friends, for when did friendship take
A breed for barren metal of his friend?
But lend it rather to thine enemy,
Who if he break, thou mayst with better face
Exact the penalty.

Shylock.
Why, look you how you storm!
I would be friends with you, and have your love,
Forget the shames that you have stain'd me with,
Supply your present wants, and take no doit
Of usance for my moneys, and you'll not hear me.
This is kind I offer.

Bassanio.
This were kindness.

Shylock.
This kindness will I show.
Go with me to a notary, seal me there
Your single bond; and in a merry sport
If you repay me not on such a day,
In such a place, such sum or sums as are
Express'd in the condition, let the forfeit
Be nominated for an equal pound
Of your fair flesh, to be cut off and taken
In what part of your body pleaseth me.

Antonio.
Content, in faith, I'll seal to such a bond,
And say there is much kindness in the Jew.

Bassanio.
You shall not seal to such a bond for me,
I'll rather dwell in my necessity.

Antonio.
Why, fear not, man, I will not forfeit it.
Within these two months, that's a month before
This bond expires, I do expect return

Of thrice three times the value of this bond.

Shylock.
O father Abram, what these Christians are,
Whose own hard dealings teaches them suspect
The thoughts of others! Pray you tell me this:
If he should break his day, what should I gain
By the exaction of the forfeiture?
A pound of man's flesh taken from a man
Is not so estimable, profitable neither,
As flesh of muttons, beefs, or goats. I say,
To buy his favor, I extend this friendship.
If he will take it, so, if not, adieu;
And for my love I pray you wrong me not.

Antonio.
Yes, Shylock, I will seal unto this bond.

Shylock.
Then meet me forthwith at the notary's;
Give him direction for this merry bond,
And I will go and purse the ducats straight,
See to my house, left in the fearful guard
Of an unthrifty knave, and presently
I'll be with you.

Exit.

Antonio.
Hie thee, gentle Jew.
The Hebrew will turn Christian, he grows kind.

Bassanio.
I like not fair terms and a villain's mind.

Antonio.
Come on, in this there can be no dismay,
My ships come home a month before the day.

ACT II

SCENE I

theme : race [handwritten in left margin]

[Flourish cornets.] Enter [the Prince of] Morocco, a tawny Moor, all in white, and three or four Followers accordingly, with Portia, Nerissa, and their Train.

Morocco.
Mislike me not for my complexion,
The shadowed livery of the burnish'd sun,
To whom I am a neighbor and near bred.
Bring me the fairest creature northward born,
Where Phoebus' fire scarce thaws the icicles,
And let us make incision for your love,
To prove whose blood is reddest, his or mine.
I tell thee, lady, this aspect of mine
Hath fear'd the valiant; by my love, I swear
The best-regarded virgins of our clime
Have lov'd it too. I would not change this hue,
Except to steal your thoughts, my gentle queen.

Portia.
In terms of choice I am not soly led
By nice direction of a maiden's eyes;

23

Besides, the lott'ry of my destiny
Bars me the right of voluntary choosing.
But if my father had not scanted me,
And hedg'd me by his wit to yield myself
His wife who wins me by that means I told you,
Yourself, renowned Prince, then stood as fair
As any comer I have look'd on yet
For my affection.

Morocco.
Even for that I thank you;
Therefore I pray you lead me to the caskets
To try my fortune. By this scimitar
That slew the Sophy and a Persian prince
That won three fields of Sultan Solyman,
I would o'erstare the sternest eyes that look,
Outbrave the heart most daring on the earth,
Pluck the young sucking cubs from the she-bear,
Yea, mock the lion when 'a roars for prey,
To win [thee], lady. But alas the while!
If Hercules and Lichas play at dice
Which is the better man, the greater throw
May turn by fortune from the weaker hand:
So is Alcides beaten by his [page],
And so may I, blind fortune leading me,
Miss that which one unworthier may attain,
And die with grieving.

Portia.
You must take your chance,
And either not attempt to choose at all,
Or swear before you choose, if you choose wrong
Never to speak to lady afterward
In way of marriage; therefore be advis'd.

Morocco.
Nor will not. Come bring me unto my chance.

Portia.
First, forward to the temple; after dinner
Your hazard shall be made.

Morocco.
Good fortune then!
To make me blest or cursed'st among men.

[Cornets.] Exeunt.

SCENE II

deciding to run away from the Jews bc he hates them

Enter the Clown [Launcelot Gobbo] alone.

Launcelot. [Certainly my conscience will serve me to 1
run from this Jew my master.]The fiend is at mine el- 2
bow and tempts me, saying to me, "[Gobbo], Launcelot
[Gobbo], good Launcelot," or "good [Gobbo]," or "good
Launcelot [Gobbo], use your legs, take the start, run
away." My conscience says, "No; take heed, honest
Launcelot, take heed, honest [Gobbo]," or as aforesaid,
"honest Launcelot [Gobbo], do not run, scorn running
with thy heels." Well, the most courageous fiend bids
me pack. "Fia!" says the fiend; "away!" says the fiend;
"for the heavens, rouse up a brave mind," says the
fiend, "and run." Well, my conscience, hanging about
the neck of my heart, says very wisely to me, "My honest friend Launcelot, being an honest man's son"—or
rather an honest woman's son, for indeed my father
did something smack, something grow to, he had a
kind of taste—well, my conscience says, "Launcelot,
bouge not." "Bouge," says the fiend. "Bouge not," says
my conscience. "Conscience," say I, "you counsel well."
"Fiend," say I, "you counsel well." To be rul'd by my
conscience, [I should stay with the Jew my master, who 21
(God bless the mark) is a kind of devil; and to run
away from the Jew, I should be rul'd by the fiend, who,
saving your reverence, is the devil himself.] Certainly 24
the Jew is the very devil incarnation, and in my con- 25

science, my conscience is but a kind of hard conscience, to offer to counsel me to stay with the Jew. The fiend gives the more friendly counsel: I will run, fiend; my heels are at your commandement, I will run.

Enter Old Gobbo with a basket.

Gobbo. Master young man, you, I pray you, which is the way to Master Jew's? 31

Launcelot. *[Aside.]* O heavens, this is my true-begotten father, who being more than sand-blind, high gravel-blind, knows me not. I will try confusions with him.

Gobbo. Master young gentleman, I pray you, which is the way to Master Jew's?

Launcelot. Turn up on your right hand at the next turning, but at the next turning of all, on your left; marry, at the very next turning, turn of no hand, but turn down indirectly to the Jew's house.

Gobbo. Be God's sonties, 'twill be a hard way to hit. Can you tell me whether one Launcelot, that dwells with him, dwell with him or no?

Launcelot. Talk you of young Master Launcelot? *[Aside.]* Mark me now, now will I raise the waters.— Talk you of young Master Launcelot?

Gobbo. No master, sir, but a poor man's son. His father, though I say't, is an honest exceeding poor man and, God be thank'd, well to live.

Launcelot. Well, let his father be what 'a will, we talk of young Master Launcelot.

Gobbo. Your worship's friend and Launcelot, sir.

Launcelot. But I pray you, ergo, old man, ergo, I beseech you, talk you of young Master Launcelot.

Gobbo. Of Launcelot, an't please your mastership.

Launcelot. Ergo, Master Launcelot. Talk not of Master Launcelot, father, for the young gentleman, according to Fates ánd Destinies, and such odd sayings, the Sisters Three, and such branches of learning, is indeed deceas'd, or as you would say in plain terms, gone to heaven.

Gobbo. Marry, God forbid, the boy was the very staff of my age, my very prop.

Launcelot. *[Aside.]* Do I look like a cudgel or a hovel-post, a staff, or a prop?—Do you know me, father?

Gobbo. Alack the day, I know you not, young gentleman, but I pray you tell me, is my boy, God rest his soul, alive or dead?

Launcelot. Do you not know me, father?

Gobbo. Alack, sir, I am sand-blind, I know you not.

Launcelot. Nay, indeed if you had your eyes you might fail of the knowing me; it is a wise father that knows his own child. Well, old man, I will tell you news of your son. Give me your blessing; truth will come to light; murder cannot be hid long; a man's son may, but in the end truth will out.

Gobbo. Pray you, sir, stand up. I am sure you are not Launcelot, my boy.

Launcelot. Pray you let's have no more fooling about it, but give me your blessing. I am Launcelot, your boy that was, your son that is, your child that shall be.

Gobbo. I cannot think you are my son.

Launcelot. I know not what I shall think of that; but I am Launcelot, the Jew's man, and I am sure Margery your wife is my mother.

Gobbo. Her name is Margery indeed. I'll be sworn, if thou be Launcelot, thou art mine own flesh and blood. Lord worshipp'd might he be, what a beard hast thou got! Thou hast got more hair on thy chin than Dobbin my fill-horse has on his tail. 91

Launcelot. It should seem then that Dobbin's tail grows backward. I am sure he had more hair of his tail than I have of my face when I [last] saw him.

Gobbo. Lord, how art thou chang'd! How dost thou and thy master agree? I have brought him a present. How 'gree you now?

Launcelot. Well, well; but for mine own part, as I have set up my rest to run away, so I will not rest till I have run some ground. My master's a very Jew. Give him a present! give him a halter. I am famish'd in his service; you may tell every finger I have with my ribs. Father, I am glad you are come; give me your present to one Master Bassanio, who indeed gives rare new liveries.] If I serve not him, I will run as far as God has any ground. O rare fortune, here comes the man. To him, father, for I am a Jew if I serve the Jew any longer.

Enter Bassanio with a follower or two, [one of them Leonardo].

Bassanio. You may do so, but let it be so hasted that supper be ready at the farthest by five of the clock. See these letters deliver'd, put the liveries to making, and desire Gratiano to come anon to my lodging.

[Exit one of his men.]

Launcelot. To him, father.

Gobbo. God bless your worship!

Bassanio. Gramercy, wouldst thou aught with me?

Gobbo. Here's my son, sir, a poor boy—

Launcelot. Not a poor boy, sir, but the rich Jew's man, that would, sir, as my father shall specify—

Gobbo. He hath a great infection, sir, as one would say, to serve—

Launcelot. Indeed the short and the long is, I serve the Jew, and have a desire, as my father shall specify—

Gobbo. His master and he (saving your worship's reverence) are scarce cater-cousins—

Launcelot. To be brief, the very truth is that the Jew, having done me wrong, doth cause me, as my father, being I hope an old man, shall frutify unto you—

Gobbo. I have here a dish of doves that I would bestow upon your worship, and my suit is—

Launcelot. In very brief, the suit is impertinent to myself, as your worship shall know by this honest old man, and though I say it, though old man, yet poor man, my father.

Bassanio. One speak for both. What would you?

Launcelot. Serve you, sir.

Gobbo. That is the very defect of the matter, sir.

Bassanio.
I know thee well, thou hast obtain'd thy suit.
Shylock thy master spoke with me this day,
And hath preferr'd thee, if it be preferment
To leave a rich Jew's service, to become
The follower of so poor a gentleman.

Launcelot. The old proverb is very well parted between my master Shylock and you, sir: you have the grace of God, sir, and he hath enough.

Bassanio.
Thou speak'st it well. Go, father, with thy son.
Take leave of thy old master, and inquire
My lodging out.—Give him a livery
More guarded than his fellows'; see it done.

Launcelot. Father, in. I cannot get a service, no, I have ne'er a tongue in my head, well! *[Looking on his palm.]* If any man in Italy have a fairer table, which doth offer to swear upon a book, I shall have good fortune. Go to, here's a simple line of life! Here's a small trifle of wives! Alas, fifteen wives is nothing! Aleven widows and nine maids is a simple coming-in for one man. And then to scape drowning thrice, and to be in peril of my life with the edge of a feather-bed, here are simple scapes. Well, if Fortune be a woman, she's a good wench for this gear. Father, come, I'll take my leave of the Jew in the twinkling.

Exit Clown [with Old Gobbo].

Bassanio.
I pray thee, good Leonardo, think on this:
These things being bought and orderly bestowed,
Return in haste, for I do feast to-night
My best esteem'd acquaintance. Hie thee, go.

Leon.
My best endeavors shall be done herein.

Enter Gratiano.

Gratiano.
Where's your master?

Leon.
Yonder, sir, he walks.

Exit Leonardo.

Gratiano.
Signior Bassanio!

Bassanio.
Gratiano!

Gratiano.
I have suit to you.

Bassanio.
You have obtain'd it.

Gratiano. You must not deny me; I must go with you to Belmont.

Bassanio.
Why then you must. But hear thee, Gratiano:
Thou art too wild, too rude, and bold of voice—
Parts that become thee happily enough,
And in such eyes as ours appear not faults,

But where thou art not known, why, there they show
Something too liberal. Pray thee take pain
To allay with some cold drops of modesty
Thy skipping spirit, lest through thy wild behavior
I be misconst'red in the place I go to,
And lose my hopes.

Gratiano.
Signior Bassanio, hear me:
If I do not put on a sober habit,
Talk with respect, and swear but now and then,
Wear prayer-books in my pocket, look demurely,
Nay more, while grace is saying hood mine eyes
Thus with my hat, and sigh and say amen,
Use all the observance of civility,
Like one well studied in a sad ostent
To please his grandam, never trust me more.

Bassanio.
Well, we shall see your bearing.

Gratiano.
Nay, but I bar to-night, you shall not gauge me
By what we do to-night.

Bassanio.
No, that were pity.
I would entreat you rather to put on
Your boldest suit of mirth, for we have friends
That purpose merriment. But fare you well,
I have some business.

Gratiano.
And I must to Lorenzo and the rest,
But we will visit you at supper-time.

Exeunt.

tonight doesn't count
have fun

SCENE III

Christian & Jew → love each other (handwritten)

Enter Jessica and the Clown [Launcelot].

Jessica.
I am sorry thou wilt leave my father so.
Our house is hell, and thou, a merry devil,
Didst rob it of some taste of tediousness.
But fare thee well, there is a ducat for thee,
And, Launcelot, soon at supper shalt thou see
Lorenzo, who is thy new master's guest.
Give him this letter, do it secretly,
And so farewell. I would not have my father
See me in talk with thee.

Launcelot. Adieu, tears exhibit my tongue. Most beau- 10
tiful pagan, most sweet Jew! if a Christian do not play 11
the knave and get thee, I am much deceiv'd. But adieu,
these foolish drops do something drown my manly spirit. Adieu!

not really (handwritten)
a Jew! you're good (handwritten)

Jessica.
Farewell, good Launcelot.

[Exit Launcelot.]

Alack, what heinous sin is it in me
To be ashamed to be my father's child!
But though I am a daughter to his blood,
I am not to his manners. O Lorenzo,
If thou keep promise, I shall end this strife,
Become a Christian and thy loving wife.

Exit.

32

SCENE IV

Lorenzo giving Jessica something

Enter Gratiano, Lorenzo, Salerio, and Solanio.

Lorenzo.
Nay, we will slink away in supper-time,
Disguise us at my lodging, and return
All in an hour.

Gratiano.
We have not made good preparation.

Salerio.
We have not spoke us yet of torch-bearers.

Solanio.
'Tis vile, unless it may be quaintly ordered,
And better in my mind not undertook.

Lorenzo.
'Tis now but four of clock, we have two hours
To furnish us.

Enter Launcelot [with a letter].
Friend Launcelot, what's the news?

Launcelot. And it shall please you to break up this, it
shall seem to signify.

Lorenzo.
I know the hand; in faith, 'tis a fair hand,
And whiter than the paper it writ on
Is the fair hand that writ.

Gratiano.
Love-news, in faith.

Launcelot. By your leave, sir.

Lorenzo. Whither goest thou?

Launcelot. Marry, sir, to bid my old master the Jew to sup to-night with my new master the Christian.

Lorenzo.
Hold here, take this. Tell gentle Jessica
I will not fail her, speak it privately.

Exit Clown.

Go, gentlemen,
Will you prepare you for this masque to-night?
I am provided of a torch-bearer.

Salerio.
Ay, marry, I'll be gone about it straight.

Solanio.
And so will I.

Lorenzo.
Meet me and Gratiano
At Gratiano's lodging some hour hence.

Salerio.
'Tis good we do so.

Exit [with Solanio].

Gratiano.
Was not that letter from fair Jessica?

Lorenzo.
I must needs tell thee all. She hath directed
How I shall take her from her father's house,
What gold and jewels she is furnish'd with,
What page's suit she hath in readiness.
If e'er the Jew her father come to heaven,
It will be for his gentle daughter's sake,
And never dare misfortune cross her foot,
Unless she do it under this excuse,
That she is issue to a faithless Jew.
Come go with me, peruse this as thou goest.
Fair Jessica shall be my torch-bearer.

Exeunt.

SCENE V

Enter [Shylock the] Jew and his man that was, the Clown [Launcelot]

Shylock.
Well, thou shalt see, thy eyes shall be thy judge,
The difference of old Shylock and Bassanio.—
What, Jessica!—Thou shalt not gurmandize,
As thou hast done with me—What, Jessica!—
And sleep and snore, and rend apparel out—
Why, Jessica, I say!

Launcelot.
Why, Jessica!

Shylock.
Who bids thee call? I do not bid thee call.

Launcelot. Your worship was wont to tell me I could do nothing without bidding.

Enter Jessica.

Jessica.
Call you? what is your will?

Shylock.
I am bid forth to supper, Jessica.
There are my keys. But wherefore should I go?
I am not bid for love, they flatter me,
But yet I'll go in hate, to feed upon
The prodigal Christian. Jessica, my girl,
Look to my house. I am right loath to go;
There is some ill a-brewing towards my rest,
For I did dream of money-bags to-night.

Launcelot. I beseech you, sir, go. My young master doth expect your reproach.

Shylock. So do I his.

Launcelot. And they have conspir'd together. I will not say you shall see a masque, but if you do, then it was not for nothing that my nose fell a-bleeding on Black Monday last at six a' clock i' th' morning, falling out that year on Ash We'n'sday was four year in th' afternoon.

Shylock.
What, are there masques? Hear you me, Jessica:
Lock up my doors, and when you hear the drum
And the vile squealing of the wry-neck'd fife,
Clamber not you up to the casements then,
Nor thrust your head into the public street
To gaze on Christian fools with varnish'd faces;
But stop my house's ears, I mean my casements;
Let not the sound of shallow fopp'ry enter
My sober house. By Jacob's staff I swear
I have no mind of feasting forth to-night;
But I will go. Go you before me, sirrah,
Say I will come.

Launcelot. I will go before, sir. Mistress, look out at window for all this—
There will come a Christian by,
Will be worth a Jewess' eye.

[Exit.]

Shylock.
What says that fool of Hagar's offspring, ha?

Jessica.
His words were "Farewell, mistress!"—nothing else.

Shylock.
The patch is kind enough, but a huge feeder,
Snail-slow in profit, and he sleeps by day
More than the wild-cat. Drones hive not with me,
Therefore I part with him, and part with him
To one that I would have him help to waste
His borrowed purse. Well, Jessica, go in,
Perhaps I will return immediately.
Do as I bid you, shut doors after you;

Fast bind, fast find—
A proverb never stale in thrifty mind.

Exit.

Jessica.
Farewell, and if my fortune be not cross'd,
I have a father, you a daughter, lost.

Exit.

SCENE VI

Enter [two of] the masquers, Gratiano and Salerio.

Gratiano.
This is the penthouse under which Lorenzo
Desir'd us to make stand.

Salerio.
His hour is almost past.

Gratiano.
And it is marvel he out-dwells his hour,
For lovers ever run before the clock.

Salerio.
O, ten times faster Venus' pigeons fly
To seal love's bonds new made, than they are wont
To keep obliged faith unforfeited!

Gratiano.
That ever holds. Who riseth from a feast
With that keen appetite that he sits down?
Where is the horse that doth untread again
His tedious measures with the unbated fire
That he did pace them first? All things that are,
Are with more spirit chased than enjoy'd.

How like a younger or a prodigal
The scarfed bark puts from her native bay,
Hugg'd and embraced by the strumpet wind!
How like the prodigal doth she return,
With over-weather'd ribs and ragged sails,
Lean, rent, and beggar'd by the strumpet wind!

Enter Lorenzo.

Salerio.
Here comes Lorenzo, more of this hereafter.

Lorenzo.
Sweet friends, your patience for my long abode;
Not I but my affairs have made you wait.
When you shall please to play the thieves for wives,
I'll watch as long for you then. Approach,
Here dwells my father Jew. Ho! who's within?

[Enter] Jessica above [in boy's clothes].

Jessica.
Who are you? tell me for more certainty,
Albeit I'll swear that I do know your tongue.

Lorenzo.
Lorenzo, and thy love.

Jessica.
Lorenzo, certain, and my love indeed,
For who love I so much? And now who knows
But you, Lorenzo, whether I am yours?

Lorenzo.
Heaven and thy thoughts are witness that thou art.

Jessica.
Here, catch this casket, it is worth the pains.
I am glad 'tis night, you do not look on me,
For I am much asham'd of my exchange.
But love is blind, and lovers cannot see
The pretty follies that themselves commit,
For if they could, Cupid himself would blush
To see me thus transformed to a boy.

Lorenzo.
Descend, for you must be my torch-bearer.

Jessica.
What, must I hold a candle to my shames?
They in themselves, good sooth, are too too light.
Why, 'tis an office of discovery, love,
And I should be obscur'd.

Lorenzo.
So are you, sweet,
Even in the lovely garnish of a boy.
But come at once,
For the close night doth play the runaway,
And we are stay'd for at Bassanio's feast.

Jessica.
I will make fast the doors, and gild myself
With some moe ducats, and be with you straight.

[Exit above.]

Gratiano.
Now by my hood, a gentle, and no Jew.

Lorenzo.
Beshrow me but I love her heartily,
For she is wise, if I can judge of her,
And fair she is, if that mine eyes be true,
And true she is, as she hath prov'd herself;
And therefore, like herself, wise, fair, and true,
Shall she be placed in my constant soul.

Enter Jessica.
What, art thou come? On, [gentlemen], away!
Our masquing mates by this time for us stay.

Exit [with Jessica and Salerio].

Enter Antonio.

Antonio.
Who's there?

Gratiano.
Signior Antonio!

Antonio.
Fie, fie, Gratiano, where are all the rest?
'Tis nine a' clock—our friends all stay for you.
No masque to-night, the wind is come about,
Bassanio presently will go aboard.
I have sent twenty out to seek for you.

Gratiano.
I am glad on't. I desire no more delight
Than to be under sail, and gone to-night.

Exeunt.

SCENE VII

*[Flourish cornets.] Enter Portia with [the Prince of]
Morocco and both their Trains.*

Portia.
Go, draw aside the curtains and discover
The several caskets to this noble prince.
Now make your choice.

Morocco.
This first, of gold, who this inscription bears,
"Who chooseth me shall gain what many men desire";
The second, silver, which this promise carries,
"Who chooseth me shall get as much as he deserves";
This third, dull lead, with warning all as blunt,
"Who chooseth me must give and hazard all he hath."
How shall I know if I do choose the right?

Portia.
The one of them contains my picture, Prince:
If you choose that, then I am yours withal.

Morocco.

Some god direct my judgment! Let me see,
I will survey th' inscriptions back again.
What says this leaden casket?
"Who chooseth me must give and hazard all he hath."
Must give—for what? for lead, hazard for lead?
This casket threatens. Men that hazard all
Do it in hope of fair advantages;
A golden mind stoops not to shows of dross.
I'll then nor give nor hazard aught for lead.
What says the silver with her virgin hue?
"Who chooseth me shall get as much as he deserves."
As much as he deserves! pause there, Morocco,
And weigh thy value with an even hand.
If thou beest rated by thy estimation,
Thou dost deserve enough, and yet enough
May not extend so far as to the lady;
And yet to be afeard of my deserving
Were but a weak disabling of myself.
As much as I deserve! why, that's the lady.
I do in birth deserve her, and in fortunes,
In graces, and in qualities of breeding;
But more than these, in love I do deserve.
What if I stray'd no farther, but chose here?
Let's see once more this saying grav'd in gold:
"Who chooseth me shall gain what many men desire."
Why, that's the lady, all the world desires her.
From the four corners of the earth they come
To kiss this shrine, this mortal breathing saint.
The Hyrcanian deserts and the vasty wilds
Of wide Arabia are as throughfares now
For princes to come view fair Portia.
The watery kingdom, whose ambitious head
Spets in the face of heaven, is no bar
To stop the foreign spirits, but they come
As o'er a brook to see fair Portia.
One of these three contains her heavenly picture.
Is't like that lead contains her? 'Twere damnation
To think so base a thought; it were too gross
To rib her cerecloth in the obscure grave.
Or shall I think in silver she's immur'd,

Being ten times undervalued to tried gold?
O sinful thought! never so rich a gem
Was set in worse than gold. They have in England
A coin that bears the figure of an angel
Stamp'd in gold, but that's insculp'd upon;
But here an angel in a golden bed
Lies all within. Deliver me the key.
Here do I choose, and thrive I as I may!

Portia.
There take it, Prince, and if my form lie there,
Then I am yours.

[He unlocks the golden casket.]

Morocco.
O hell! what have we here?
A carrion Death, within whose empty eye
There is a written scroll! I'll read the writing.

[Reads.]
"All that glisters is not gold,
Often have you heard that told;
Many a man his life hath sold
But my outside to behold.
Gilded [tombs] do worms infold.
Had you been as wise as bold,
Young in limbs, in judgment old,
Your answer had not been inscroll'd.
Fare you well, your suit is cold."
Cold indeed, and labor lost:
Then farewell heat, and welcome frost!
Portia, adieu. I have too griev'd a heart
To take a tedious leave; thus losers part.

Exit [with his Train].

Portia.
A gentle riddance. Draw the curtains, go.
Let all of his complexion choose me so.

Exeunt.

SCENE VIII

Enter Salerio and Solanio.

Salerio.
Why, man, I saw Bassanio under sail,
With him is Gratiano gone along;
And in their ship I am sure Lorenzo is not.

Solanio.
The villain Jew with outcries rais'd the Duke,
Who went with him to search Bassanio's ship.

Salerio.
He came too late, the ship was under sail,
But there the Duke was given to understand
That in a gondilo were seen together
Lorenzo and his amorous Jessica.
Besides, Antonio certified the Duke
They were not with Bassanio in his ship.

Solanio.
I never heard a passion so confus'd,
So strange, outrageous, and so variable
As the dog Jew did utter in the streets.
"My daughter! O my ducats! O my daughter!
Fled with a Christian! O my Christian ducats!
Justice! the law! my ducats, and my daughter!
A sealed bag, two sealed bags of ducats,
Of double ducats, stol'n from me by my daughter!
And jewels, two stones, two rich and precious stones,
Stol'n by my daughter! Justice! find the girl,
She hath the stones upon her, and the ducats."

Salerio.
Why, all the boys in Venice follow him,
Crying, his stones, his daughter, and his ducats.

Solanio.

Let good Antonio look he keep his day,
Or he shall pay for this.

Salerio.

Marry, well rememb'red.
I reason'd with a Frenchman yesterday,
Who told me, in the Narrow Seas that part
The French and English, there miscarried
A vessel of our country richly fraught.
I thought upon Antonio when he told me,
And wish'd in silence that it were not his.

Solanio.

You were best to tell Antonio what you hear,
Yet do not suddenly, for it may grieve him.

Salerio.

A kinder gentleman treads not the earth.
I saw Bassanio and Antonio part:
Bassanio told him he would make some speed
Of his return; he answered, "Do not so,
[Slubber] not business for my sake, Bassanio,
But stay the very riping of the time;
And for the Jew's bond which he hath of me,
Let it not enter in your mind of love.
Be merry, and employ your chiefest thoughts
To courtship, and such fair ostents of love
As shall conveniently become you there."
And even there, his eye being big with tears,
Turning his face, he put his hand behind him,
And with affection wondrous sensible
He wrung Bassanio's hand, and so they parted.

Solanio.

I think he only loves the world for him.
I pray thee let us go and find him out
And quicken his embraced heaviness
With some delight or other.

Salerio.

Do we so.

SCENE IX

Enter Nerissa and a Servitor.

Nerissa.
Quick, quick, I pray thee, draw the curtain straight;
The Prince of Arragon hath ta'en his oath,
And comes to his election presently.

*[Flourish cornets.] Enter [the Prince of] Arragon, his
Train, and Portia.*

Portia.
Behold, there stand the caskets, noble Prince
If you choose that wherein I am contain'd,
Straight shall our nuptial rites be solemniz'd;
But if you fail, without more speech, my lord,
You must be gone from hence immediately.

Arragon.
I am enjoin'd by oath to observe three things:
First, never to unfold to any one
Which casket 'twas I chose; next, if I fail
Of the right casket, never in my life
To woo a maid in way of marriage;
Lastly,
If I do fail in fortune of my choice,
Immediately to leave you, and be gone.

Portia.
To these injunctions every one doth swear
That comes to hazard for my worthless self.

Arragon.
And so have I address'd me. Fortune now
To my heart's hope! Gold, silver, and base lead.
"Who chooseth me must give and hazard all he hath."
You shall look fairer ere I give or hazard.

What says the golden chest? Ha, let me see:
"Who chooseth me shall gain what many men desire."
What many men desire! That many may be meant
By the fool multitude that choose by show,
Not learning more than the fond eye doth teach,
Which pries not to th' interior, but like the martlet
Builds in the weather on the outward wall,
Even in the force and road of casualty.
I will not choose what many men desire,
Because I will not jump with common spirits,
And rank me with the barbarous multitudes.
Why then to thee, thou silver treasure house,
Tell me once more what title thou dost bear:
"Who chooseth me shall get as much as he deserves."
And well said too; for who shall go about
To cozen fortune, and be honorable
Without the stamp of merit? Let none presume
To wear an undeserved dignity.
O that estates, degrees, and offices
Were not deriv'd corruptly, and that clear honor
Were purchas'd by the merit of the wearer!
How many then should cover that stand bare?
How many be commanded that command?
How much low peasantry would then be gleaned
From the true seed of honor? and how much honor
Pick'd from the chaff and ruin of the times
To be new varnish'd? Well, but to my choice:
"Who chooseth me shall get as much as he deserves."
I will assume desert. Give me a key for this,
And instantly unlock my fortunes here.

[He unlocks the silver casket.]

Portia.
Too long a pause for that which you find there.

Arragon.
What's here? the portrait of a blinking idiot,
Presenting me a schedule! I will read it.
How much unlike art thou to Portia!
How much unlike my hopes and my deservings!
"Who chooseth me shall have as much as he deserves"!

Did I deserve no more than a fool's head?
Is that my prize? Are my deserts no better?

Portia.
To offend and judge are distinct offices,
And of opposed natures.

Arragon.
What is here?

[Reads.]
"The fire seven times tried this:
Seven times tried that judgment is,
That did never choose amiss.
Some there be that shadows kiss,
Such have but a shadow's bliss.
There be fools alive, iwis,
Silver'd o'er, and so was this.
Take what wife you will to bed,
I will ever be your head.
So be gone, you are sped."
Still more fool I shall appear
By the time I linger here.
With one fool's head I came to woo,
But I go away with two.
Sweet, adieu. I'll keep my oath,
Patiently to bear my wroth.

[Exit with his Train.]

Portia.
Thus hath the candle sing'd the moth.
O, these deliberate fools, when they do choose,
They have the wisdom by their wit to lose.

Nerissa.
The ancient saying is no heresy,
Hanging and wiving goes by destiny.

Portia.
Come draw the curtain, Nerissa.

Enter Messenger.

Messenger.
Where is my lady?

Portia.
Here; what would my lord?

Messenger.
Madam, there is alighted at your gate
A young Venetian, one that comes before
To signify th' approaching of his lord,
From whom he bringeth sensible regreets:
To wit (besides commends and courteous breath),
Gifts of rich value. Yet I have not seen
So likely an embassador of love.
A day in April never came so sweet,
To show how costly summer was at hand,
As this fore-spurrer comes before his lord.

Portia.
No more, I pray thee. I am half afeard
Thou wilt say anon he is some kin to thee,
Thou spend'st such high-day wit in praising him.
Come, come, Nerissa, for I long to see
Quick Cupid's post that comes so mannerly.

Nerissa.
Bassanio, Lord Love, if thy will it be!

Exeunt.

ACT III

Antisemitism (handwritten)

Antonio's ship down (handwritten)

Shylock's daughter spent his money (handwritten)

SCENE I

[Enter] Solanio and Salerio.

Solanio. Now what news on the Rialto?

Salerio. Why, yet it lives there uncheck'd that Antonio hath a ship of rich lading wrack'd on the Narrow Seas; the Goodwins I think they call the place, a very dangerous flat, and fatal, where the carcasses of many a tall ship lie buried, as they say, if my gossip Report be an honest woman of her word.

Solanio. I would she were as lying a gossip in that as ever knapp'd ginger or made her neighbors believe she wept for the death of a third husband. But it is true, without any slips of prolixity, or crossing the plain highway of talk, that the good Antonio, the honest Antonio—O that I had a title good enough to keep his name company!—

Salerio. Come, the full stop.

Solanio. Ha, what sayest thou? Why, the end is, he hath lost a ship.

17 (handwritten)

Salerio. I would it might prove the end of his losses.

Solanio. Let me say amen betimes, lest the devil cross my prayer, for here he comes in the likeness of a Jew.

Enter Shylock.

How now, Shylock, what news among the merchants?

Shylock. You knew, none so well, none so well as you, of my daughter's flight.

Salerio. That's certain. I for my part knew the tailor that made the wings she flew withal.

Solanio. And Shylock for his own part knew the bird was flidge, and then it is the complexion of them all to leave the dam.

Shylock. She is damn'd for it.

Salerio. That's certain, if the devil may be her judge.

Shylock. My own flesh and blood to rebel!

Solanio. Out upon it, old carrion, rebels it at these years? *too old to feel frisky*

Shylock. I say, my daughter is my flesh and my blood.

Salerio. There is more difference between thy flesh and hers than between jet and ivory, more between your bloods than there is between red wine and Rhenish. But tell us, do you hear whether Antonio have had any loss at sea or no?

Shylock. There I have another bad match. A bankrout, a prodigal, who dare scarce show his head on the Rialto; a beggar, that was us'd to come so smug upon the mart: let him look to his bond. He was wont to call me usurer, let him look to his bond. He was wont to lend money for a Christian cur'sy, let him look to his bond.

Salerio. Why, I am sure if he forfeit thou wilt not take his flesh. What's that good for?

[handwritten margin note: humorous relief]

Shylock. To bait fish withal—if it will feed nothing 48 else, it will feed my revenge. He hath disgrac'd me, and hind'red me half a million, laugh'd at my losses, mock'd at my gains, scorn'd my nation, thwarted my bargains, cool'd my friends, heated mine enemies; and what's his reason? I am a Jew. Hath not a Jew eyes? 53 Hath not a Jew hands, organs, dimensions, senses, affections, passions; fed with the same food, hurt with the same weapons, subject to the same diseases, heal'd by the same means, warm'd and cool'd by the same winter and summer, as a Christian is? If you prick us, 58 do we not bleed? If you tickle us, do we not laugh? If you poison us, do we not die? And if you wrong us, 60 shall we not revenge? If we are like you in the rest, we will resemble you in that. If a Jew wrong a Christian, what is his humility? Revenge. If a Christian wrong a Jew, what should his sufferance be by Christian example? Why, revenge. The villainy you teach me, I will execute, and it shall go hard but I will better the instruction. 67

Enter a [Serving]man from Antonio.

Servingman. Gentlemen, my master Antonio is at his house, and desires to speak with you both.

Salerio. We have been up and down to seek him.

Enter Tubal.

Solanio. Here comes another of the tribe; a third cannot be match'd, unless the devil himself turn Jew.

Exeunt Gentlemen [Solanio and Salerio, with Servingman].

Shylock. How now, Tubal, what news from Genoa? Hast thou found my daughter?

Tubal. I often came where I did hear of her, but cannot find her.

Shylock. Why, there, there, there, there! A diamond gone, cost me two thousand ducats in Frankford! The curse never fell upon our nation till now, I never felt it till now. Two thousand ducats in that, and other precious, precious jewels. I would my daughter were dead at my foot, and the jewels in her ear! Would she were hears'd at my foot, and the ducats in her coffin! No news of them? Why, so—and I know not what's spent in the search. Why, thou loss upon loss! the thief gone with so much, and so much to find the thief, and no satisfaction, no revenge, nor no ill luck stirring but what lights a' my shoulders, no sighs but a' my breathing, no tears but a' my shedding.

Tubal. Yes, other men have ill luck too. Antonio, as I heard in Genoa—

Shylock. What, what, what? ill luck, ill luck?

Tubal. Hath an argosy cast away, coming from Tripolis.

Shylock. I thank God, I thank God. Is it true, is it true?

Tubal. I spoke with some of the sailors that escap'd the wrack.

Shylock. I thank thee, good Tubal, good news, good news! Ha, ha! [Heard] in Genoa?

Tubal. Your daughter spent in Genoa, as I heard, one night fourscore ducats.

Shylock. Thou stick'st a dagger in me. I shall never see my gold again. Fourscore ducats at a sitting, fourscore ducats!

Tubal. There came divers of Antonio's creditors in my company to Venice that swear he cannot choose but break.

Shylock. I am very glad of it. I'll plague him, I'll torture him. I am glad of it.

Tubal. One of them show'd me a ring that he had of your daughter for a monkey.

Shylock. Out upon her! Thou torturest me, Tubal. It was my turkis, I had it of Leah when I was a bachelor. I would not have given it for a wilderness of monkeys.

Tubal. But Antonio is certainly undone.

Shylock. Nay, that's true, that's very true. Go, Tubal, fee me an officer; bespeak him a fortnight before. I will have the heart of him if he forfeit, for were he out of Venice I can make what merchandise I will. Go, Tubal, and meet me at our synagogue; go, good Tubal, at our synagogue, Tubal.

Exeunt.

SCENE II

Enter Bassanio, Portia, Gratiano, [Nerissa,] and all their Trains.

Portia.
I pray you tarry, pause a day or two
Before you hazard, for in choosing wrong
I lose your company; therefore forbear a while.
There's something tells me (but it is not love)
I would not lose you, and you know yourself,
Hate counsels not in such a quality.
But lest you should not understand me well—
And yet a maiden hath no tongue but thought—
I would detain you here some month or two
Before you venture for me. I could teach you
How to choose right, but then I am forsworn.
So will I never be, so may you miss me,

But if you do, you'll make me wish a sin,
That I had been forsworn. Beshrow your eyes,
They have o'erlook'd me and divided me:
One half of me is yours, the other half yours—
Mine own, I would say; but if mine, then yours,
And so all yours. O, these naughty times
Puts bars between the owners and their rights!
And so though yours, not yours. Prove it so,
Let fortune go to hell for it, not I.
I speak too long, but 'tis to peize the time,
To eche it, and to draw it out in length,
To stay you from election.

Bassanio.

Let me choose,
For as I am, I live upon the rack.

Portia.

Upon the rack, Bassanio! then confess
What treason there is mingled with your love.

Bassanio.

None but that ugly treason of mistrust,
Which makes me fear th' enjoying of my love;
There may as well be amity and life
'Tween snow and fire, as treason and my love.

Portia.

Ay, but I fear you speak upon the rack,
Where men enforced do speak any thing.

Bassanio.

Promise me life, and I'll confess the truth.

Portia.

Well then, confess and live.

Bassanio.

Confess and love
Had been the very sum of my confession.
O happy torment, when my torturer
Doth teach me answers for deliverance!
But let me to my fortune and the caskets.

Portia.

Away then! I am lock'd in one of them;
If you do love me, you will find me out.
Nerissa and the rest, stand all aloof.
Let music sound while he doth make his choice;
Then if he lose he makes a swan-like end,
Fading in music. That the comparison
May stand more proper, my eye shall be the stream
And wat'ry death-bed for him. He may win,
And what is music then? Then music is
Even as the flourish when true subjects bow
To a new-crowned monarch; such it is
As are those dulcet sounds in break of day
That creep into the dreaming bridegroom's ear,
And summon him to marriage. Now he goes,
With no less presence, but with much more love,
Than young Alcides, when he did redeem
The virgin tribute paid by howling Troy
To the sea-monster. I stand for sacrifice;
The rest aloof are the Dardanian wives,
With bleared visages, come forth to view
The issue of th' exploit. Go, Hercules,
Live thou, I live; with much, much more dismay
I view the fight than thou that mak'st the fray.

[Here music.]

*A song, the whilst Bassanio comments on the caskets
to himself.*

Tell me where is fancy bred,
Or in the heart or in the head?
How begot, how nourished?

All.

Reply, reply.
It is engend'red in the [eyes],
With gazing fed, and fancy dies
In the cradle where it lies.
Let us all ring fancy's knell.
I'll begin it.Ding, dong, bell.

All.

Ding, dong, bell.

55

Bassanio.
So may the outward shows be least themselves—
The world is still deceiv'd with ornament.
In law, what plea so tainted and corrupt
But, being season'd with a gracious voice,
Obscures the show of evil? In religion,
What damned error but some sober brow
Will bless it, and approve it with a text,
Hiding the grossness with fair ornament?
There is no [vice] so simple but assumes
Some mark of virtue on his outward parts.
How many cowards, whose hearts are all as false
As stairs of sand, wear yet upon their chins
The beards of Hercules and frowning Mars,
Who inward search'd, have livers white as milk,
And these assume but valor's excrement
To render them redoubted! Look on beauty,
And you shall see 'tis purchas'd by the weight,
Which therein works a miracle in nature,
Making them lightest that wear most of it.
So are those crisped snaky golden locks,
Which [make] such wanton gambols with the wind
Upon supposed fairness, often known
To be the dowry of a second head,
The skull that bred them in the sepulchre.
Thus ornament is but the guiled shore
To a most dangerous sea; the beauteous scarf
Veiling an Indian beauty; in a word,
The seeming truth which cunning times put on
To entrap the wisest. Therefore then, thou gaudy gold,
Hard food for Midas, I will none of thee;
Nor none of thee, thou pale and common drudge
'Tween man and man; but thou, thou meagre lead,
Which rather threaten'st than dost promise aught,
Thy paleness moves me more than eloquence,
And here choose I. Joy be the consequence!

Chooses lead

Portia. *[Aside.]*
How all the other passions fleet to air,
As doubtful thoughts, and rash-embrac'd despair,
And shudd'ring fear, and green-eyed jealousy!

O love, be moderate, allay thy ecstasy,
In measure rain thy joy, scant this excess!
I feel too much thy blessing; make it less,
For fear I surfeit.

Bassanio.
What find I here?

[Opening the leaden casket.]
Fair Portia's counterfeit! What demigod
Hath come so near creation? Move these eyes?
Or whether, riding on the balls of mine,
Seem they in motion? Here are sever'd lips,
Parted with sugar breath; so sweet a bar
Should sunder such sweet friends. Here in her hairs
The painter plays the spider, and hath woven
A golden mesh t' entrap the hearts of men
Faster than gnats in cobwebs. But her eyes—
How could he see to do them? Having made one,
Methinks it should have power to steal both his
And leave itself unfurnish'd. Yet look how far
The substance of my praise doth wrong this shadow
In underprizing it, so far this shadow
Doth limp behind the substance. Here's the scroll,
The continent and summary of my fortune.

[Reads.]
"You that choose not by the view,
Chance as fair, and choose as true:
Since this fortune falls to you,
Be content, and seek no new.
If you be well pleas'd with this,
And hold your fortune for your bliss,
Turn you where your lady is,
And claim her with a loving kiss."
A gentle scroll. Fair lady, by your leave,
I come by note, to give and to receive.
Like one of two contending in a prize,
That thinks he hath done well in people's eyes,
Hearing applause and universal shout,
Giddy in spirit, still gazing in a doubt
Whether those peals of praise be his or no,

So, thrice-fair lady, stand I, even so,
As doubtful whether what I see be true,
Until confirm'd, sign'd, ratified by you.

Portia.

You see me, Lord Bassanio, where I stand,
Such as I am. Though for myself alone
I would not be ambitious in my wish
To wish myself much better, yet for you,
I would be trebled twenty times myself,
A thousand times more fair, ten thousand times more rich,
That only to stand high in your account,
I might in virtues, beauties, livings, friends,
Exceed account. But the full sum of me
Is sum of something; which, to term in gross,
Is an unlesson'd girl, unschool'd, unpractic'd,
Happy in this, she is not yet so old
But she may learn; happier than this,
She is not bred so dull but she can learn;
Happiest of all, is that her gentle spirit
Commits itself to yours to be directed,
As from her lord, her governor, her king.
Myself, and what is mine, to you and yours
Is now converted. But now I was the lord
Of this fair mansion, master of my servants,
Queen o'er myself; and even now, but now,
This house, these servants, and this same myself
Are yours—my lord's!—I give them with this ring,
Which when you part from, lose, or give away,
Let it presage the ruin of your love,
And be my vantage to exclaim on you.

Bassanio.

Madam, you have bereft me of all words,
Only my blood speaks to you in my veins,
And there is such confusion in my powers,
As after some oration fairly spoke
By a beloved prince, there doth appear
Among the buzzing pleased multitude,
Where every something, being blent together,
Turns to a wild of nothing, save of joy
Express'd and not express'd. But when this ring

Parts from this finger, then parts life from hence;
O then be bold to say Bassanio's dead!

Nerissa.
My lord and lady, it is now our time,
That have stood by and seen our wishes prosper,
To cry good joy. Good joy, my lord and lady!

Gratiano.
My Lord Bassanio and my gentle lady,
I wish you all the joy that you can wish;
For I am sure you can wish none from me;
And when your honors mean to solemnize
The bargain of your faith, I do beseech you
Even at that time I may be married too.

Bassanio.
With all my heart, so thou canst get a wife.

Gratiano.
I thank your lordship, you have got me one.
My eyes, my lord, can look as swift as yours:
You saw the mistress, I beheld the maid;
You lov'd, I lov'd; for intermission
No more pertains to me, my lord, than you;
Your fortune stood upon the caskets there,
And so did mine too as the matter falls;
For wooing here until I sweat again,
And swearing till my very [roof] was dry
With oaths of love, at last, if promise last,
I got a promise of this fair one here
To have her love—provided that your fortune
Achiev'd her mistress.

Portia.
Is this true, Nerissa?

Nerissa.
Madam, it is, so you stand pleas'd withal.

Bassanio.
And do you, Gratiano, mean good faith?

Gratiano.
Yes, faith, my lord.

Bassanio.
Our feast shall be much honored in your marriage.

Gratiano. We'll play with them the first boy for a thousand ducats.

Nerissa. What, and stake down?

Gratiano. No, we shall ne'er win at that sport, and stake down.
But who comes here? Lorenzo and his infidel? *Jessica*
What, and my old Venetian friend Salerio?

Enter Lorenzo, Jessica, and Salerio, a messenger from Venice.

Bassanio.
Lorenzo and Salerio, welcome hither,
If that the youth of my new int'rest here
Have power to bid you welcome. By your leave,
I bid my very friends and countrymen,
Sweet Portia, welcome.

Portia.
So do I, my lord,
They are entirely welcome.

Lorenzo.
I thank your honor. For my part, my lord,
My purpose was not to have seen you here,
But meeting with Salerio by the way,
He did entreat me, past all saying nay,
To come with him along.

Salerio.
I did, my lord,
And I have reason for it. Signior Antonio
Commends him to you.

- *[Gives Bassanio a letter.]*

Bassanio.
Ere I ope his letter,

I pray you tell me how my good friend doth.

Salerio.
Not sick, my lord, unless it be in mind,
Nor well, unless in mind. His letter there
Will show you his estate.

[Bassanio] open the letter.

Gratiano.
Nerissa, cheer yond stranger, bid her welcome.
Your hand, Salerio. What's the news from Venice?
How doth that royal merchant, good Antonio?
I know he will be glad of our success;
We are the Jasons, we have won the fleece.

Salerio.
I would you had won the fleece that he hath lost.

Portia.
There are some shrowd contents in yond same paper
That steals the color from Bassanio's cheek—
Some dear friend dead, else nothing in the world
Could turn so much the constitution
Of any constant man. What, worse and worse!
With leave, Bassanio, I am half yourself,
And I must freely have the half of any thing
That this same paper brings you.

Bassanio.
O sweet Portia,
Here are a few of the unpleasant'st words
That ever blotted paper! Gentle lady,
When I did first impart my love to you,
I freely told you all the wealth I had
Ran in my veins: I was a gentleman;
And then I told you true. And yet, dear lady,
Rating myself at nothing, you shall see
How much I was a braggart: when I told you
My state was nothing, I should then have told you
That I was worse than nothing; for indeed
I have engag'd myself to a dear friend,
Engag'd my friend to his mere enemy,
To feed my means. Here is a letter, lady,

The paper as the body of my friend,
And every word in it a gaping wound
Issuing life-blood. But is it true, Salerio?
Hath all his ventures fail'd? What, not one hit?
From Tripolis, from Mexico, and England,
From Lisbon, Barbary, and India,
And not one vessel scape the dreadful touch
Of merchant-marring rocks?

Salerio.

Not one, my lord.
Besides, it should appear, that if he had
The present money to discharge the Jew,
He would not take it. Never did I know
A creature that did bear the shape of man
So keen and greedy to confound a man.
He plies the Duke at morning and at night,
And doth impeach the freedom of the state,
If they deny him justice. Twenty merchants,
The Duke himself, and the magnificoes
Of greatest port, have all persuaded with him,
But none can drive him from the envious plea
Of forfeiture, of justice, and his bond.

Jessica.

When I was with him I have heard him swear
To Tubal and to Chus, his countrymen,
That he would rather have Antonio's flesh
Than twenty times the value of the sum
That he did owe him; and I know, my lord,
If law, authority, and power deny not,
It will go hard with poor Antonio.

Portia.

Is it your dear friend that is thus in trouble?

Bassanio.

The dearest friend to me, the kindest man,
The best-condition'd and unwearied spirit
In doing courtesies, and one in whom
The ancient Roman honor more appears
Than any that draws breath in Italy.

Portia.

What sum owes he the Jew?

Bassanio.

For me, three thousand ducats.

Portia.

What, no more?
Pay him six thousand, and deface the bond;
Double six thousand, and then treble that,
Before a friend of this description
Shall lose a hair through Bassanio's fault.
First go with me to church and call me wife,
And then away to Venice to your friend;
For never shall you lie by Portia's side
With an unquiet soul. You shall have gold
To pay the petty debt twenty times over.
When it is paid, bring your true friend along.
My maid Nerissa and myself mean time
Will live as maids and widows. Come away!
For you shall hence upon your wedding-day.
Bid your friends welcome, show a merry cheer—
Since you are dear bought, I will love you dear.
But let me hear the letter of your friend.

[**Bassanio.** *(Reads.)*] "Sweet Bassanio, my ships have all miscarried, my creditors grow cruel, my estate is very low, my bond to the Jew is forfeit; and since in paying it, it is impossible I should live, all debts are clear'd between you and I, if I might but see you at my death. Notwithstanding, use your pleasure; if your love do not persuade you to come, let not my letter."

Portia.

O love! dispatch all business and be gone.

Bassanio.

Since I have your good leave to go away,
I will make haste; but till I come again,
No bed shall e'er be guilty of my stay,
Nor rest be interposer 'twixt us twain.

Exeunt.

SCENE III

*Enter [Shylock] the Jew and [Solanio] and Antonio
and the Jailer.*

Shylock.
Jailer, look to him, tell not me of mercy.
This is the fool that lent out money gratis.
Jailer, look to him.

Antonio.
Hear me yet, good Shylock.

Shylock.
I'll have my bond, speak not against my bond,
I have sworn an oath that I will have my bond.
Thou call'dst me dog before thou hadst a cause,
But since I am a dog, beware my fangs.
The Duke shall grant me justice. I do wonder,
Thou naughty jailer, that thou art so fond
To come abroad with him at his request.

Antonio.
I pray thee hear me speak.

Shylock.
I'll have my bond; I will not hear thee speak.
I'll have my bond, and therefore speak no more.
I'll not be made a soft and dull-ey'd fool
To shake the head, relent, and sigh, and yield
To Christian intercessors. Follow not,
I'll have no speaking, I will have my bond.

Exit Jew.

Solanio.
It is the most impenetrable cur
That ever kept with men.

Antonio.
Let him alone,
I'll follow him no more with bootless prayers.
He seeks my life; his reason well I know:
I oft deliver'd from his forfeitures
Many that have at times made moan to me;
Therefore he hates me.

[Solanio.]
I am sure the Duke
Will never grant this forfeiture to hold.

Antonio.
The Duke cannot deny the course of law;
For the commodity that strangers have
With us in Venice, if it be denied,
Will much impeach the justice of the state,
Since that the trade and profit of the city
Consisteth of all nations. Therefore go.
These griefs and losses have so bated me
That I shall hardly spare a pound of flesh
To-morrow to my bloody creditor.
Well, jailer, on. Pray God Bassanio come
To see me pay his debt, and then I care not!

Exeunt.

SCENE IV

Enter Portia, Nerissa, Lorenzo, Jessica, and [Balthazar,] a man of Portia's.

Lorenzo.
Madam, although I speak it in your presence,
You have a noble and a true conceit
Of godlike amity, which appears most strongly

In bearing thus the absence of your lord.
But if you knew to whom you show this honor,
How true a gentleman you send relief,
How dear a lover of my lord your husband,
I know you would be prouder of the work
Than customary bounty can enforce you.

Portia.

I never did repent for doing good,
Nor shall not now: for in companions
That do converse and waste the time together,
Whose souls do bear an egall yoke of love,
There must be needs a like proportion
Of lineaments, of manners, and of spirit;
Which makes me think that this Antonio,
Being the bosom lover of my lord,
Must needs be like my lord. If it be so,
How little is the cost I have bestowed
In purchasing the semblance of my soul,
From out the state of hellish cruelty.
This comes too near the praising of myself,
Therefore no more of it. [Hear] other things:
Lorenzo, I commit into your hands
The husbandry and manage of my house
Until my lord's return. For mine own part,
I have toward heaven breath'd a secret vow
To live in prayer and contemplation,
Only attended by Nerissa here,
Until her husband and my lord's return.
There is a monast'ry two miles off,
And there we will abide. I do desire you
Not to deny this imposition,
The which my love and some necessity
Now lays upon you.

Lorenzo.

Madam, with all my heart,
I shall obey you in all fair commands.

Portia.

My people do already know my mind,
And will acknowledge you and Jessica

In place of Lord Bassanio and myself.
So fare you well till we shall meet again.

Lorenzo.
Fair thoughts and happy hours attend on you!

Jessica.
I wish your ladyship all heart's content.

Portia.
I thank you for your wish, and am well pleas'd
To wish it back on you. Fare you well, Jessica.

Exeunt [Jessica and Lorenzo].
Now, Balthazar,
As I have ever found thee honest-true,
So let me find thee still. Take this same letter,
And use thou all th' endeavor of a man
In speed to [Padua]. See thou render this
Into my [cousin's] hands, Doctor Bellario,
And look what notes and garments he doth give thee,
Bring them, I pray thee, with imagin'd speed
Unto the [traject], to the common ferry
Which trades to Venice. Waste no time in words,
But get thee gone. I shall be there before thee.

Balthazar.
Madam, I go with all convenient speed.

[Exit.]

Portia.
Come on, Nerissa, I have work in hand
That you yet know not of. We'll see our husbands
Before they think of us.

Nerissa.
Shall they see us?

Portia.
They shall, Nerissa; but in such a habit
That they shall think we are accomplished
With that we lack. I'll hold thee any wager,
When we are both accoutered like young men,
I'll prove the prettier fellow of the two,

And wear my dagger with the braver grace,
And speak between the change of man and boy
With a reed voice, and turn two mincing steps
Into a manly stride; and speak of frays
Like a fine bragging youth, and tell quaint lies,
How honorable ladies sought my love,
Which I denying, they fell sick and died.
I could not do withal. Then I'll repent,
And wish, for all that, that I had not kill'd them;
And twenty of these puny lies I'll tell,
That men shall swear I have discontinued school
Above a twelvemonth. I have within my mind
A thousand raw tricks of these bragging Jacks,
Which I will practice.

Nerissa.
Why, shall we turn to men?

Portia.
Fie, what a question's that,
If thou wert near a lewd interpreter!
But come, I'll tell thee all my whole device
When I am in my coach, which stays for us
At the park-gate; and therefore haste away,
For we must measure twenty miles to-day.

Exeunt.

SCENE V

Enter Clown [Launcelot] and Jessica.

Launcelot. Yes, truly, for look you, the sins of the father are to be laid upon the children; therefore, I promise you, I fear you. I was always plain with you, and so now I speak my agitation of the matter; therefore be a' good cheer, for truly I think you are damn'd. There is but one hope in it that can do you any good, and that is but a kind of bastard hope neither.

Jessica. And what hope is that, I pray thee?

Launcelot. Marry, you may partly hope that your father got you not, that you are not the Jew's daughter.

Jessica. That were a kind of bastard hope indeed; so the sins of my mother should be visited upon me.

Launcelot. Truly then I fear you are damn'd both by father and mother; thus when I shun Scylla, your father, I fall into Charybdis, your mother. Well, you are gone both ways.

Jessica. I shall be sav'd by my husband, he hath made me a Christian!

Launcelot. Truly, the more to blame he; we were Christians enow before, e'en as many as could well live one by another. This making of Christians will raise the price of hogs. If we grow all to be pork- we shall not shortly have a rasher on the coals for money.

Enter Lorenzo.

Jessica. I'll tell my husband, Launcelot, what you say. Here he [comes].

Lorenzo. I shall grow jealous of you shortly, Launcelot, if you thus get my wife into corners!

Jessica. Nay, you need not fear us, Lorenzo, Launcelot and I are out. He tells me flatly there's no mercy for me in heaven because I am a Jew's daughter; and he says you are no good member of the commonwealth, for in converting Jews to Christians, you raise the price of pork.

Lorenzo. I shall answer that better to the commonwealth than you can the getting up of the Negro's belly; the Moor is with child by you, Launcelot.

Launcelot. It is much that the Moor should be more than reason; but if she be less than an honest woman, she is indeed more than I took her for.

Lorenzo. How every fool can play upon the word! I think the best grace of wit will shortly turn into silence, and discourse grow commendable in none only but parrots. Go in, sirrah, bid them prepare for dinner.

Launcelot. That is done, sir, they have all stomachs!

Lorenzo. Goodly Lord, what a wit-snapper are you! then bid them prepare dinner.

Launcelot. That is done too, sir, only 'cover' is the word.

Lorenzo. Will you cover then, sir?

Launcelot. Not so, sir, neither, I know my duty.

Lorenzo. Yet more quarrelling with occasion! wilt thou show the whole wealth of thy wit in an instant? I pray thee understand a plain man in his plain meaning: go to thy fellows, bid them cover the table, serve in the meat, and we will come in to dinner.

Launcelot. For the table, sir, it shall be serv'd in; for the meat, sir, it shall be cover'd; for your coming in to dinner, sir, why, let it be as humors and conceits shall govern.

Exit Clown.

Lorenzo.
O dear discretion, how his words are suited!
The fool hath planted in his memory
An army of good words, and I do know
A many fools, that stand in better place,
Garnish'd like him, that for a tricksy word
Defy the matter. How cheer'st thou, Jessica?
And now, good sweet, say thy opinion,
How dost thou like the Lord Bassanio's wife?

Jessica.
Past all expressing. It is very meet
The Lord Bassanio live an upright life,
For having such a blessing in his lady,
He finds the joys of heaven here on earth,
And if on earth he do not [merit] it,
In reason he should never come to heaven!
Why, if two gods should play some heavenly match,
And on the wager lay two earthly women,
And Portia one, there must be something else
Pawn'd with the other, for the poor rude world
Hath not her fellow.

Lorenzo.
Even such a husband
Hast thou of me as she is for [a] wife.

Jessica.
Nay, but ask my opinion too of that.

Lorenzo.
I will anon, first let us go to dinner.

Jessica.
Nay, let me praise you while I have a stomach.

Lorenzo.
No, pray thee, let it serve for table-talk;
Then howsome'er thou speak'st, 'mong other things
I shall disgest it.

Jessica.
Well, I'll set you forth.

Exeunt.

ACT IV

SCENE I

Enter the Duke, the Magnificoes, Antonio, Bassanio,
[Salerio,] and Gratiano [with others]

Duke.
What, is Antonio here?

Antonio.
Ready, so please your Grace.

Duke.
I am sorry for thee. Thou art come to answer
A stony adversary, an inhuman wretch, 4
Uncapable of pity, void and empty
From any dram of mercy.

Antonio.
I have heard
Your Grace hath ta'en great pains to qualify
His rigorous course; but since he stands obdurate,
And that no lawful means can carry me
Out of his envy's reach, I do oppose
My patience to his fury, and am arm'd 12

To suffer, with a quietness of spirit,
The very tyranny and rage of his.

Duke.
Go one, and call the Jew into the court.

Salerio.
He is ready at the door; he comes, my lord.

Enter Shylock.

Duke.
Make room, and let him stand before our face.
Shylock, the world thinks, and I think so too,
That thou but leadest this fashion of thy malice
To the last hour of act, and then 'tis thought
Thou'lt show thy mercy and remorse more strange
Than is thy strange apparent cruelty;
And where thou now exacts the penalty,
Which is a pound of this poor merchant's flesh,
Thou wilt not only loose the forfeiture,
But touch'd with humane gentleness and love,
Forgive a moi'ty of the principal,
Glancing an eye of pity on his losses,
That have of late so huddled on his back,
Enow to press a royal merchant down,
And pluck commiseration of [his state]
From brassy bosoms and rough hearts of flints,
From stubborn Turks, and Tartars never train'd
To offices of tender courtesy.
35 We all expect a gentle answer, Jew!   *play on "gentile"*

Shylock.
I have possess'd your Grace of what I purpose,
And by our holy Sabaoth have I sworn
To have the due and forfeit of my bond.
If you deny it, let the danger light
Upon your charter and your city's freedom!
You'll ask me why I rather choose to have
A weight of carrion flesh than to receive
Three thousand ducats. I'll not answer that;
But say it is my humor, is it answer'd?
45 What if my house be troubled with a rat,

And I be pleas'd to give ten thousand ducats
To have it ban'd? What, are you answer'd yet?
Some men there are love not a gaping pig;
Some that are mad if they behold a cat;
And others, when the bagpipe sings i' th' nose,
Cannot contain their urine: for affection,
[Mistress] of passion, sways it to the mood
Of what it likes or loathes. Now for your answer:
As there is no firm reason to be rend'red
Why he cannot abide a gaping pig;
Why he, a harmless necessary cat;
Why he, a woollen bagpipe, but of force
Must yield to such inevitable shame
As to offend, himself being offended;
So can I give no reason, nor I will not,
More than a lodg'd hate and a certain loathing
I bear Antonio, that I follow thus
A losing suit against him. Are you answered?

Bassanio.
This is no answer, thou unfeeling man,
To excuse the current of thy cruelty.

Shylock.
I am not bound to please thee with my answers.

Bassanio.
Do all men kill the things they do not love?

Shylock.
Hates any man the thing he would not kill?

Bassanio.
Every offense is not a hate at first.

Shylock.
What, wouldst thou have a serpent sting thee twice?

Antonio.
I pray you think you question with the Jew:
You may as well go stand upon the beach
And bid the main flood bate his usual height;
You may as well use question with the wolf
Why he hath made the ewe bleak for the lamb; 75

You may as well forbid the mountain pines
To wag their high tops, and to make no noise
When they are fretten with the gusts of heaven;
You may as well do any thing most hard
As seek to soften that—than which what's harder?—
His Jewish heart! Therefore I do beseech you
Make no moe offers, use no farther means,
But with all brief and plain conveniency
Let me have judgment and the Jew his will.

Bassanio.
For thy three thousand ducats here is six.

Shylock.
If every ducat in six thousand ducats
Were in six parts, and every part a ducat,
I would not draw them, I would have my bond.

Duke.
How shalt thou hope for mercy, rend'ring none?

Shylock.
What judgment shall I dread, doing no wrong?
You have among you many a purchas'd slave,
Which like your asses, and your dogs and mules,
You use in abject and in slavish parts,
Because you bought them. Shall I say to you,
"Let them be free! Marry them to your heirs!
Why sweat they under burthens? Let their beds
Be made as soft as yours, and let their palates
Be season'd with such viands"? You will answer,
"The slaves are ours." So do I answer you:
The pound of flesh which I demand of him
Is dearly bought as mine, and I will have it.
If you deny me, fie upon your law!
There is no force in the decrees of Venice.
I stand for judgment. Answer—shall I have it?

Duke.
Upon my power I may dismiss this court,
Unless Bellario, a learned doctor,
Whom I have sent for to determine this,
Come here to-day.

76

Salerio.

My lord, here stays without
A messenger with letters from the doctor,
New come from Padua.

Duke.

Bring us the letters; call the messenger.

Bassanio.

Good cheer, Antonio! what, man, courage yet!
The Jew shall have my flesh, blood, bones, and all,
Ere thou shalt lose for me one drop of blood.

Antonio.

I am a tainted wether of the flock,
Meetest for death; the weakest kind of fruit
Drops earliest to the ground, and so let me.
You cannot better be employ'd, Bassanio,
Than to live still and write mine epitaph.

Enter Nerissa [dressed like a lawyer's clerk].

Duke.

Came you from Padua, from Bellario?

Nerissa.

From both, my lord. Bellario greets your Grace.

[Presenting a letter.]

Bassanio.

Why dost thou whet thy knife so earnestly?

Shylock.

To cut the forfeiture from that bankrout there.

Gratiano.

Not on thy sole, but on thy soul, harsh Jew,
Thou mak'st thy knife keen; but no metal can,
No, not the hangman's axe, bear half the keenness
Of thy sharp envy. Can no prayers pierce thee?

Shylock.

No, none that thou hast wit enough to make.

77

Gratiano.

dehumanizing

130 O, be thou damn'd, inexecrable dog!
And for thy life let justice be accus'd.
Thou almost mak'st me waver in my faith
To hold opinion with Pythagoras,
That souls of animals infuse themselves
135 Into the trunks of men. Thy currish spirit
136 Govern'd a wolf, who hang'd for human slaughter,
Even from the gallows did his fell soul fleet,
And whilst thou layest in thy unhallowed dam,
Infus'd itself in thee; for thy desires
Are wolvish, bloody, starv'd, and ravenous.

animal

Shylock.

Till thou canst rail the seal from off my bond,
Thou but offend'st thy lungs to speak so loud.
Repair thy wit, good youth, or it will fall
To cureless ruin. I stand here for law.

Duke.

This letter from Bellario doth commend
A young and learned doctor to our court.
Where is he?

Nerissa.

He attendeth here hard by
To know your answer, whether you'll admit him.

Duke.

With all my heart. Some three or four of you
Go give him courteous conduct to this place.
Mean time the court shall hear Bellario's letter.

[Reads.]

"Your Grace shall understand that at the receipt of your
letter I am very sick, but in the instant that your messenger came, in loving visitation was with me a young
doctor of Rome. His name is Balthazar. I acquainted
him with the cause in controversy between the Jew and
Antonio the merchant. We turn'd o'er many books together. He is furnish'd with my opinion, which better'd
with his own learning, the greatness whereof I cannot
enough commend, comes with him, at my importunity,

to fill up your Grace's request in my stead. I beseech you let his lack of years be no impediment to let him lack a reverend estimation, for I never knew so young a body with so old a head. I leave him to your gracious acceptance, whose trial shall better publish his commendation."

Enter Portia for Balthazar.

You hear the learn'd Bellario, what he writes,
And here I take it is the doctor come.
Give me your hand. Come you from old Bellario?

Portia.
I did, my lord.

Duke.
You are welcome, take your place.
Are you acquainted with the difference
That holds this present question in the court?

Portia.
I am informed throughly of the cause.
Which is the merchant here? and which the Jew?

Duke.
Antonio and old Shylock, both stand forth.

Portia.
Is your name Shylock?

Shylock.
Shylock is my name.

Portia.
Of a strange nature is the suit you follow,
Yet in such rule that the Venetian law
Cannot impugn you as you do proceed.—
You stand within his danger, do you not?

Antonio.
Ay, so he says.

Portia.
Do you confess the bond?

Antonio.

I do.

Portia.

Then must the Jew be merciful.

Shylock.

On what compulsion must I? tell me that.

Portia.

The quality of mercy is not strain'd,
It droppeth as the gentle rain from heaven
Upon the place beneath. It is twice blest:
It blesseth him that gives and him that takes.
'Tis mightiest in the mightiest, it becomes
The thronèd monarch better than his crown.
His sceptre shows the force of temporal power,
The attribute to awe and majesty,
Wherein doth sit the dread and fear of kings;
But mercy is above this sceptred sway,
It is enthroned in the hearts of kings,
It is an attribute to God himself;
And earthly power doth then show likest God's
When mercy seasons justice. Therefore, Jew,
Though justice be thy plea, consider this,
That in the course of justice, none of us
Should see salvation. We do pray for mercy,
And that same prayer doth teach us all to render
The deeds of mercy. I have spoke thus much
To mitigate the justice of thy plea,
Which if thou follow, this strict court of Venice
Must needs give sentence 'gainst the merchant there.

Shylock.

My deeds upon my head! I crave the law,
The penalty and forfeit of my bond.

Portia.

Is he not able to discharge the money?

Bassanio.

Yes, here I tender it for him in the court,
Yea, twice the sum. If that will not suffice,
I will be bound to pay it ten times o'er,

On forfeit of my hands, my head, my heart.
If this will not suffice, it must appear
That malice bears down truth.

[To the Duke.]

And I beseech you
Wrest once the law to your authority:
To do a great right, do a little wrong,
And curb this cruel devil of his will.

Portia.
It must not be, there is no power in Venice
Can alter a decree established.
'Twill be recorded for a precedent,
And many an error by the same example
Will rush into the state. It cannot be.

Shylock.
A Daniel come to judgment! yea, a Daniel!
O wise young judge, how I do honor thee!

Portia.
I pray you let me look upon the bond.

Shylock.
Here 'tis, most reverend doctor, here it is.

Portia.
Shylock, there's thrice thy money off'red thee.

Shylock.
An oath, an oath, I have an oath in heaven!
Shall I lay perjury upon my soul?
[No], not for Venice.

Portia.
Why, this bond is forfeit,
And lawfully by this the Jew may claim
A pound of flesh, to be by him cut off
Nearest the merchant's heart. Be merciful,
Take thrice thy money, bid me tear the bond.

Shylock.
When it is paid according to the tenure.
It doth appear you are a worthy judge;

You know the law, your exposition
Hath been most sound. I charge you by the law,
Whereof you are a well-deserving pillar,
Proceed to judgment. By my soul I swear
There is no power in the tongue of man
To alter me: I stay here on my bond.

Antonio.
Most heartily I do beseech the court
To give the judgment.

Portia.
Why then thus it is:
You must prepare your bosom for his knife—

Shylock.
O noble judge, O excellent young man!

Portia.
For the intent and purpose of the law
Hath full relation to the penalty,
Which here appeareth due upon the bond.

Shylock.
'Tis very true. O wise and upright judge!
How much more elder art thou than thy looks!

Portia.
Therefore lay bare your bosom.

Shylock.
Ay, his breast,
So says the bond, doth it not, noble judge?
"Nearest his heart," those are the very words.

Portia.
It is so. Are there balance here to weigh
The flesh?

Shylock.
I have them ready.

Portia.
Have by some surgeon, Shylock, on your charge,
To stop his wounds, lest he do bleed to death.

Shylock.

Is it so nominated in the bond?

Portia.

It is not so express'd, but what of that?
'Twere good you do so much for charity.

Shylock.

I cannot find it, 'tis not in the bond.

Portia.

You, merchant, have you any thing to say?

Antonio.

But little; I am arm'd and well prepar'd.
Give me your hand, Bassanio, fare you well.
Grieve not that I am fall'n to this for you;
For herein Fortune shows herself more kind
Than is her custom. It is still her use
To let the wretched man outlive his wealth,
To view with hollow eye and wrinkled brow
An age of poverty; from which ling'ring penance
Of such misery doth she cut me off.
Commend me to your honorable wife,
Tell her the process of Antonio's end,
Say how I lov'd you, speak me fair in death;
And when the tale is told, bid her be judge
Whether Bassanio had not once a love.
Repent but you that you shall lose your friend,
And he repents not that he pays your debt;
For if the Jew do cut but deep enough,
I'll pay it instantly with all my heart.

Bassanio.

Antonio, I am married to a wife
Which is as dear to me as life itself,
But life itself, my wife, and all the world,
Are not with me esteem'd above thy life.
I would lose all, ay, sacrifice them all
Here to this devil, to deliver you.

Portia.

Your wife would give you little thanks for that
If she were by to hear you make the offer.

Gratiano.
I have a wife who I protest I love;
I would she were in heaven, so she could
Entreat some power to change this currish Jew.

Nerissa.
'Tis well you offer it behind her back,
The wish would make else an unquiet house.

1.Shylock. *[Aside.]*
These be the Christian husbands. I have a daughter—
Would any of the stock of Barrabas
Had been her husband rather than a Christian!
— We trifle time. I pray thee pursue sentence.

Portia.
A pound of that same merchant's flesh is thine,
The court awards it, and the law doth give it.

Shylock.
Most rightful judge!

Portia.
And you must cut this flesh from off his breast,
The law allows it, and the court awards it.

Shylock.
Most learned judge, a sentence! Come prepare!

Portia.
Tarry a little, there is something else.
This bond doth give thee here no jot of blood;
The words expressly are 'a pound of flesh.'
Take then thy bond, take thou thy pound of flesh,
But in the cutting it, if thou dost shed
One drop of Christian blood, thy lands and goods
Are by the laws of Venice confiscate
Unto the state of Venice.

Gratiano.
O upright judge! Mark, Jew. O learned judge!

Shylock.
Is that the law?

Portia.

Thyself shalt see the act;
For as thou urgest justice, be assur'd
Thou shalt have justice more than thou desir'st.

Gratiano.

O learned judge! Mark, Jew, a learned judge!

Shylock.

I take this offer then; pay the bond thrice
And let the Christian go.

Bassanio.

Here is the money.

Portia.

Soft,
The Jew shall have all justice. Soft, no haste.
He shall have nothing but the penalty.

Gratiano.

O Jew! an upright judge, a learned judge!

Portia.

Therefore prepare thee to cut off the flesh.
Shed thou no blood, nor cut thou less nor more
But just a pound of flesh. If thou tak'st more
Or less than a just pound, be it but so much
As makes it light or heavy in the substance
Or the division of the twentith part
Of one poor scruple, nay, if the scale do turn
But in the estimation of a hair,
Thou diest, and all thy goods are confiscate.

Gratiano.

A second Daniel! a Daniel, Jew!
Now, infidel, I have you on the hip.

Portia.

Why doth the Jew pause? Take thy forfeiture.

Shylock.

Give me my principal, and let me go.

Bassanio.

I have it ready for thee, here it is.

Portia.

He hath refus'd it in the open court;
He shall have merely justice and his bond.

Gratiano.

A Daniel, still say I, a second Daniel!
I thank thee, Jew, for teaching me that word.

Shylock.

Shall I not have barely my principal?

Portia.

Thou shalt have nothing but the forfeiture,
To be so taken at thy peril, Jew.

Shylock.

Why then the devil give him good of it!
I'll stay no longer question.

Portia.

Tarry, Jew,
The law hath yet another hold on you.
It is enacted in the laws of Venice,
If it be proved against an alien,
That by direct or indirect attempts
He seek the life of any citizen,
The party 'gainst the which he doth contrive
Shall seize one half his goods; the other half
Comes to the privy coffer of the state,
And the offender's life lies in the mercy
Of the Duke only, 'gainst all other voice:
In which predicament I say thou stand'st;
For it appears, by manifest proceeding,
That indirectly, and directly too,
Thou hast contrived against the very life
Of the defendant; and thou hast incurr'd
The danger formerly by me rehears'd.
Down therefore, and beg mercy of the Duke.

Gratiano.

Beg that thou mayst have leave to hang thyself,

And yet thy wealth being forfeit to the state,
Thou hast not left the value of a cord;
Therefore thou must be hang'd at the state's charge.

Duke.
That thou shalt see the difference of our spirit,
I pardon thee thy life before thou ask it.
For half thy wealth, it is Antonio's;
The other half comes to the general state,
Which humbleness may drive unto a fine.

Portia.
Ay, for the state, not for Antonio.

Shylock.
366 [Nay, take my life and all, pardon not that:]
You take my house when you do take the prop
That doth sustain my house; you take my life
When you do take the means whereby I live.

*might as well
condemn me
to death*

Portia.
What mercy can you render him, Antonio?

Gratiano.
A halter gratis—nothing else, for God sake.

Antonio.
So please my lord the Duke and all the court
To quit the fine for one half of his goods,
I am content; so he will let me have
The other half in use, to render it
Upon his death unto the gentleman
That lately stole his daughter.
Two things provided more, that for this favor
399 He presently become a Christian;
400 The other, that he do record a gift,
Here in the court, of all he dies possess'd
Unto his son Lorenzo and his daughter.

*force him to convert
& strip him of Jewish
identity*

Duke.
He shall do this, or else I do recant
The pardon that I late pronounced here.
404

are you happy now?

Portia.
Art thou contented, Jew? what dost thou say?

Shylock.
I am content.

Portia.
Clerk, draw a deed of gift.

Shylock.
I pray you give me leave to go from hence,
I am not well. Send the deed after me,
And I will sign it.

Duke.
Get thee gone, but do it.

[Gratiano.]
In christ'ning shalt thou have two god-fathers:
Had I been judge, thou shouldst have had ten more,
To bring thee to the gallows, not to the font.

Exit [Shylock].

Duke.
Sir, I entreat you home with me to dinner.

Portia.
I humbly do desire your Grace of pardon,
I must away this night toward Padua,
And it is meet I presently set forth.

Duke.
I am sorry that your leisure serves you not.
Antonio, gratify this gentleman,
For in my mind you are much bound to him.

Exeunt Duke and his Train.

Bassanio.
Most worthy gentleman, I and my friend
Have by your wisdom been this day acquitted
Of grievous penalties, in lieu whereof
Three thousand ducats, due unto the Jew,
We freely cope your courteous pains withal.

Antonio.
And stand indebted, over and above,
In love and service to you evermore.

Portia.
He is well paid that is well satisfied,
And I, delivering you, am satisfied,
And therein do account myself well paid.
My mind was never yet more mercenary.
I pray you know me when we meet again;
I wish you well, and so I take my leave.

Bassanio.
Dear sir, of force I must attempt you further.
Take some remembrance of us as a tribute,
Not as fee. Grant me two things, I pray you,
Not to deny me, and to pardon me.

Portia.
You press me far, and therefore I will yield.

[To Antonio.]
Give me your gloves, I'll wear them for your sake,

[To Bassanio.]
And for your love I'll take this ring from you.
Do not draw back your hand, I'll take no more,
And you in love shall not deny me this!

Bassanio.
This ring, good sir, alas, it is a trifle!
I will not shame myself to give you this.

Portia.
I will have nothing else but only this,
And now methinks I have a mind to it.

Bassanio.
There's more depends on this than on the value.
The dearest ring in Venice will I give you,
And find it out by proclamation;
Only for this, I pray you pardon me.

Portia.
I see, sir, you are liberal in offers.

You taught me first to beg, and now methinks
You teach me how a beggar should be answer'd.

Bassanio.
Good sir, this ring was given me by my wife,
And when she put it on, she made me vow
That I should neither sell, nor give, nor lose it.

Portia.
That 'scuse serves many men to save their gifts,
And if your wife be not a mad woman,
And know how well I have deserv'd this ring,
She would not hold out enemy for ever
For giving it to me. Well, peace be with you!

Exeunt [Portia and Nerissa].

Antonio.
My Lord Bassanio, let him have the ring.
Let his deservings and my love withal
Be valued 'gainst your wive's commandement.

Bassanio.
Go, Gratiano, run and overtake him;
Give him the ring, and bring him, if thou canst,
Unto Antonio's house. Away, make haste.

Exit Gratiano.
Come, you and I will thither presently,
And in the morning early will we both
Fly toward Belmont. Come, Antonio.

Exeunt.

SCENE II

Enter [Portia and] Nerissa [disguised as before]

Portia.
Inquire the Jew's house out, give him this deed,
And let him sign it. We'll away to-night,
And be a day before our husbands home.
This deed will be well welcome to Lorenzo.

Enter Gratiano.

Gratiano.
Fair sir, you are well o'erta'en.
My Lord Bassanio upon more advice
Hath sent you here this ring, and doth entreat
Your company at dinner.

Portia.
That cannot be.
His ring I do accept most thankfully,
And so I pray you tell him; furthermore,
I pray you show my youth old Shylock's house.

Gratiano.
That will I do.

Nerissa.
Sir, I would speak with you.

[Aside to Portia.]
I'll see if I can get my husband's ring,
Which I did make him swear to keep for ever.

Portia. *[Aside to Nerissa.]*
Thou mayst, I warrant. We shall have old swearing
That they did give the rings away to men;
But we'll outface them, and outswear them too.—
Away, make haste. Thou know'st where I will tarry.

Nerissa.
Come, good sir, will you show me to this house?

[Exeunt.]

ACT V

SCENE I

Enter Lorenzo and Jessica.

Lorenzo.
The moon shines bright. In such a night as this,
When the sweet wind did gently kiss the trees,
And they did make no noise, in such a night
Troilus methinks mounted the Troyan walls,
And sigh'd his soul toward the Grecian tents,
Where Cressid lay that night.

Jessica.
In such a night
Did Thisby fearfully o'ertrip the dew,
And saw the lion's shadow ere himself,
And ran dismayed away.

Lorenzo.
In such a night
Stood Dido with a willow in her hand
Upon the wild sea-banks, and waft her love
To come again to Carthage.

Jessica.
In such a night
Medea gathered the enchanted herbs
That did renew old Aeson.

Lorenzo.
In such a night
Did Jessica steal from the wealthy Jew,
And with an unthrift love did run from Venice,
As far as Belmont.

Jessica.
In such a night
Did young Lorenzo swear he lov'd her well,
Stealing her soul with many vows of faith,
And ne'er a true one.

Lorenzo.
In such a night
Did pretty Jessica (like a little shrow)
Slander her love, and he forgave it her.

Jessica.
I would out-night you, did nobody come;
But hark, I hear the footing of a man.

Enter a Messenger.

Lorenzo.
Who comes so fast in silence of the night?

Messenger.
A friend.

Lorenzo.
A friend! what friend? your name, I pray you, friend?

Messenger.
Stephano is my name, and I bring word
My mistress will before the break of day
Be here at Belmont. She doth stray about
By holy crosses, where she kneels and prays
For happy wedlock hours.

Lorenzo.
Who comes with her?

Messenger.
None but a holy hermit and her maid.
I pray you, is my master yet return'd?

Lorenzo.
He is not, nor we have not heard from him.
But go we in, I pray thee, Jessica,
And ceremoniously let us prepare
Some welcome for the mistress of the house.

Enter Clown [Launcelot].

Launcelot. Sola, sola! wo ha, ho! sola, sola!

Lorenzo. Who calls?

Launcelot. Sola! did you see Master Lorenzo? Master Lorenzo, sola, sola!

Lorenzo. Leave hollowing, man—here.

Launcelot. Sola! where, where?

Lorenzo. Here!

Launcelot. Tell him there's a post come from my master, with his horn full of good news. My master will be here ere morning.

[Exit.]

Lorenzo.
Sweet soul, let's in, and there expect their coming.
And yet no matter; why should we go in?
My friend [Stephano], signify, I pray you,
Within the house, your mistress is at hand,
And bring your music forth into the air.

[Exit Messenger.]
How sweet the moonlight sleeps upon this bank!
Here will we sit, and let the sounds of music
Creep in our ears. Soft stillness and the night
Become the touches of sweet harmony.
Sit, Jessica. Look how the floor of heaven

Is thick inlaid with patens of bright gold.
There's not the smallest orb which thou behold'st
But in his motion like an angel sings,
Still quiring to the young-ey'd cherubins;
Such harmony is in immortal souls,
But whilst this muddy vesture of decay
Doth grossly close it in, we cannot hear it.

[Enter Musicians.]
Come ho, and wake Diana with a hymn,
With sweetest touches pierce your mistress' ear,
And draw her home with music.

Play Music.

Jessica.
I am never merry when I hear sweet music.

Lorenzo.
The reason is, your spirits are attentive;
For do but note a wild and wanton herd
Or race of youthful and unhandled colts,
Fetching mad bounds, bellowing and neighing loud,
Which is the hot condition of their blood,
If they but hear perchance a trumpet sound,
Or any air of music touch their ears,
You shall perceive them make a mutual stand,
Their savage eyes turn'd to a modest gaze,
By the sweet power of music; therefore the poet
Did feign that Orpheus drew trees, stones, and floods;
Since nought so stockish, hard, and full of rage,
But music for the time doth change his nature.
The man that hath no music in himself,
Nor is not moved with concord of sweet sounds,
Is fit for treasons, stratagems, and spoils;
The motions of his spirit are dull as night,
And his affections dark as [Erebus]
Let no such man be trusted. Mark the music.

Enter Portia and Nerissa.

Portia.
That light we see is burning in my hall.
How far that little candle throws his beams!

So shines a good deed in a naughty world.

Nerissa.
When the moon shone, we did not see the candle.

Portia.
So doth the greater glory dim the less:
A substitute shines brightly as a king
Until a king be by, and then his state
Empties itself, as doth an inland brook
Into the main of waters. Music, hark!

Nerissa.
It is your music, madam, of the house.

Portia.
Nothing is good, I see, without respect;
Methinks it sounds much sweeter than by day.

Nerissa.
Silence bestows that virtue on it, madam.

Portia.
The crow doth sing as sweetly as the lark
When neither is attended; and I think
The nightingale, if she should sing by day
When every goose is cackling, would be thought
No better a musician than the wren.
How many things by season season'd are
To their right praise and true perfection!
Peace ho! the Moon sleeps with Endymion,
And would not be awak'd.

[Music ceases.]

Lorenzo.
That is the voice,
Or I am much deceiv'd, of Portia.

Portia.
He knows me as the blind man knows the cuckoo,
By the bad voice!

Lorenzo.
Dear lady, welcome home!

Portia.
We have been praying for our husbands' welfare,
Which speed we hope the better for our words.
Are they return'd?

Lorenzo.
Madam, they are not yet;
But there is come a messenger before,
To signify their coming.

Portia.
Go in, Nerissa.
Give order to my servants that they take
No note at all of our being absent hence—
Nor you, Lorenzo—Jessica, nor you.

[A tucket sounds.]

Lorenzo.
Your husband is at hand, I hear his trumpet.
We are no tell-tales, madam, fear you not.

Portia.
This night methinks is but the daylight sick,
It looks a little paler. 'Tis a day,
Such as the day is when the sun is hid.

*Enter Bassanio, Antonio, Gratiano, and their Fol-
lowers.*

Bassanio.
We should hold day with the Antipodes,
If you would walk in absence of the sun.

Portia.
Let me give light, but let me not be light,
For a light wife doth make a heavy husband,
And never be Bassanio so for me—
But God sort all! You are welcome home, my lord.

Bassanio.
I thank you, madam. Give welcome to my friend;
This is the man, this is Antonio,
To whom I am so infinitely bound.

Portia.
You should in all sense be much bound to him,
For as I hear he was much bound for you.

Antonio.
No more than I am well acquitted of.

Portia.
Sir, you are very welcome to our house.
It must appear in other ways than words,
Therefore I scant this breathing courtesy.

Gratiano. *[To Nerissa.]*
By yonder moon I swear you do me wrong;
In faith, I gave it to the judge's clerk.
Would he were gelt that had it, for my part,
Since you do take it, love, so much at heart.

Portia.
A quarrel ho already! what's the matter?

Gratiano.
About a hoop of gold, a paltry ring
That she did give me, whose posy was
For all the world like cutler's poetry
Upon a knife, "Love me, and leave me not."

Nerissa.
What talk you of the posy or the value?
You swore to me, when I did give [it] you,   150
That you would wear it till your hour of death,
And that it should lie with you in your grave.
Though not for me, yet for your vehement oaths,
You should have been respective and have kept it.
Gave it a judge's clerk! no, God's my judge,
The clerk will ne'er wear hair on 's face that had it.

Gratiano.
He will, and if he live to be a man.

Nerissa.
Ay, if a woman live to be a man.

Gratiano.
Now, by this hand, I gave it to a youth,

160 A kind of boy, a little scrubbed boy,
No higher than thyself, the judge's clerk,
A prating boy, that begg'd it as a fee.
I could not for my heart deny it him.

Portia.
You were to blame, I must be plain with you,
To part so slightly with your wive's first gift,
A thing stuck on with oaths upon your finger,
And so riveted with faith unto your flesh.
I gave my love a ring, and made him swear
Never to part with it, and here he stands.
I dare be sworn for him he would not leave it,
Nor pluck it from his finger, for the wealth
That the world masters. Now, in faith, Gratiano,
You give your wife too unkind a cause of grief;
And 'twere to me I should be mad at it.

Bassanio. *[Aside.]*
Why, I were best to cut my left hand off,
And swear I lost the ring defending it.

Gratiano.
My Lord Bassanio gave his ring away
Unto the judge that begg'd it, and indeed
Deserv'd it too; and then the boy, his clerk,
That took some pains in writing, he begg'd mine,
And neither man nor master would take aught
But the two rings.

Portia.
What ring gave you, my lord?
Not that, I hope, which you receiv'd of me.

Bassanio.
If I could add a lie unto a fault,
I would deny it; but you see my finger
Hath not the ring upon it, it is gone.

Portia.
Even so void is your false heart of truth.
By heaven, I will ne'er come in your bed
Until I see the ring!

Nerissa.
Nor I in yours
Till I again see mine!

Bassanio.
Sweet Portia,
If you did know to whom I gave the ring,
If you did know for whom I gave the ring,
And would conceive for what I gave the ring,
And how unwillingly I left the ring,
When nought would be accepted but the ring,
You would abate the strength of your displeasure.

Portia.
200 If you had known the virtue of the ring,
Or half her worthiness that gave the ring,
Or your own honor to contain the ring,
You would not then have parted with the ring.
What man is there so much unreasonable,
If you had pleas'd to have defended it
With any terms of zeal, wanted the modesty
To urge the thing held as a ceremony?
Nerissa teaches me what to believe—
I'll die for't but some woman had the ring!

Bassanio.
No, by my honor, madam, by my soul,
No woman had it, but a civil doctor,
Which did refuse three thousand ducats of me,
And begg'd the ring, the which I did deny him,
And suffer'd him to go displeas'd away—
Even he that had held up the very life
Of my dear friend. What should I say, sweet lady?
I was enforc'd to send it after him,
I was beset with shame and courtesy,
My honor would not let ingratitude
So much besmear it. Pardon me, good lady,
For by these blessed candles of the night,
Had you been there, I think you would have begg'd
The ring of me to give the worthy doctor.

Portia.
Let not that doctor e'er come near my house.

Since he hath got the jewel that I loved,
And that which you did swear to keep for me,
I will become as liberal as you,
I'll not deny him any thing I have,
No, not my body nor my husband's bed.
Know him I shall, I am well sure of it.
Lie not a night from home. Watch me like Argus;
If you do not, if I be left alone,
Now by mine honor, which is yet mine own,
I'll have that doctor for [my] bedfellow.

Nerissa. *what are you gonna do for me?*
And I his clerk; therefore be well advis'd
How you do leave me to mine own protection.

Gratiano.
Well, do you so; let not me take him then,
For if I do, I'll mar the young clerk's pen.

Antonio.
I am th' unhappy subject of these quarrels.

Portia.
Sir, grieve not you, you are welcome notwithstanding.

Bassanio.
Portia, forgive me this enforced wrong,
And in the hearing of these many friends
I swear to thee, even by thine own fair eyes,
Wherein I see myself—

Portia.
Mark you but that!
In both my eyes he doubly sees himself,
In each eye, one. Swear by your double self,
And there's an oath of credit.

Bassanio.
Nay, but hear me.
Pardon this fault, and by my soul I swear
I never more will break an oath with thee.

Antonio.
I once did lend my body for his wealth,

Which but for him that had your husband's ring
Had quite miscarried. I dare be bound again, 254
My soul upon the forfeit, that your lord
Will never more break faith advisedly.

Portia.

Then you shall be his surety. Give him this,
And bid him keep it better than the other.

Antonio.

Here, Lord Bassanio, swear to keep this ring.

Bassanio.

By heaven, it is the same I gave the doctor!

Portia.

I had it of him. Pardon me, Bassanio,
For by this ring, the doctor lay with me.

Nerissa.

And pardon me, my gentle Gratiano,
For that same scrubbed boy, the doctor's clerk,
In lieu of this last night did lie with me.

Gratiano.

Why, this is like the mending of highways
In summer, where the ways are fair enough.
What, are we cuckolds ere we have deserv'd it?

Portia.

Speak not so grossly, you are all amaz'd.
Here is a letter, read it at your leisure.
It comes from Padua, from Bellario.
There you shall find that Portia was the doctor,
Nerissa there her clerk. Lorenzo here
Shall witness I set forth as soon as you,
And even but now return'd; I have not yet
Enter'd my house. Antonio, you are welcome,
And I have better news in store for you
Than you expect. Unseal this letter soon; 278
There you shall find three of your argosies
Are richly come to harbor suddenly.
You shall not know by what strange accident
I chanced on this letter.

Antonio.
I am dumb.

Bassanio.
Were you the doctor, and I knew you not?

Gratiano.
Were you the clerk that is to make me cuckold?

Nerissa.
Ay, but the clerk that never means to do it,
Unless he live until he be a man.

Bassanio.
Sweet doctor, you shall be my bedfellow—
When I am absent, then lie with my wife.

Antonio.
Sweet lady, you have given me life and living,
For here I read for certain that my ships
Are safely come to road.

Portia.
How now, Lorenzo?
My clerk hath some good comforts too for you.

Nerissa.
Ay, and I'll give them him without a fee.
There do I give to you and Jessica,
From the rich Jew, a special deed of gift,
After his death, of all he dies possess'd of.

Lorenzo.
Fair ladies, you drop manna in the way
Of starved people.

Portia.
It is almost morning,
And yet I am sure you are not satisfied
Of these events at full. Let us go in,
And charge us there upon inter'gatories,
And we will answer all things faithfully.

Gratiano.
Let it be so. The first inter'gatory

That my Nerissa shall be sworn on is,
Whether till the next night she had rather stay,
Or go to bed now, being two hours to day.
But were the day come, I should wish it dark
Till I were couching with the doctor's clerk.
Well, while I live I'll fear no other thing
So sore, as keeping safe Nerissa's ring.

Exeunt.

pacing, flustered
waiting for her chance to speak

Made in the USA
San Bernardino, CA
19 January 2020